Do you hunt ghosts wearing sheets,

Or the ones that used to be people?

Bridging the Gap Between Mediumship & Paranormal Investigation

Susan Stush

RPSS Publishing - Buffalo, New York

Any resemblance to persons living or dead should be plainly apparent to them and those who know them, especially since the author has been kind enough to have provided their real names. You know who you are..

All events described herein actually happened, though on occasion the author has taken certain, very small, liberties with chronology, because she just wanted to.

Dedicated to my niece, Tess.
If not for you, I would not have
ever considered this journey.

By the way, the answer to your
question is "both."

CONTENTS

INTRODUCTION

It was Christmas. My family was gathered at my sister's home celebrating the Season and enjoying our annual holiday feast. Suddenly, my youngest niece Tess puts down her fork and looks me straight in the eye and says, "Aunt Sue, when you do that ghost hunting thing, do you hunt the type of ghosts that wear sheets or the ones that used to be people?" There was dead silence at the table, no pun intended. There she sat, drilling a hole in my forehead with her stare and waiting patiently for an answer. I met her gaze and stated, "I'll have to get back to you on that." Until now, I never did.

Here's the situation. I'm a paranormal investigator and medium. I love this more than anything in the world – either world, take your pick. My family, on the other hand chooses to ignore this fact, and treats it as the proverbial elephant in the living room. In fact, I spend most of my time pushing the envelope with my husband, who I sometimes envision coming at me with the rest of the family yelling "Get the net!". I will always be grateful to my niece for breaking that silence and inspiring me to write this book. My road exploring the supernatural has been a bit like the Yellow Brick Road; long, rambling and full of surprises, sans flying monkeys. I began taking mediumship workshops and courses in a place called Lily Dale. Those in the Western New York area and who are in the Spiritualist community know it well. It is the birthplace of Spiritualism and is "World's Largest Center for the Science Philosophy and Religion of Spiritualism". Every summer Lily Dale throws open her doors and offers workshops and classes on a variety of esoteric subjects, but in those days, only for a brief 10-week period. Thanks to COVID, we now have Zoom. I have been privileged to meet and study with some wonderful people and meet great friends and incredibly gifted mediums throughout the years. Unfortunately, after that 10-week period, the cold Western New York winter would blow into town and things get a bit desolate. Driving is a nightmare and I live an hour away. Most of my acquaintances live in different areas of the country, so I would go through this dry spell of limited contact with our circle of friends and the afterlife.

So there I was, sulking in the dark days of winter, when I found an interesting website for a group of paranormal investigators in my area. I had no idea who they were, what their philosophy was or even what they were trying to achieve.

My first thought was, "Wow! I talk to dead people, they talk to dead people…it doesn't get much better than that!" Hoping for the best, I left a message on their website that I was a medium and would very much enjoy tagging along on an investigation. If there is one thing I have learned is that there are no coincidences and Spirit will provide what is needed.

Time passes with no response. I arrived home from work one evening and my husband informs me someone named Jerry from a "para/county group-something" called and would like me to return the call. I was elated! The saga will continue throughout these chapters. It is my wish for this book to explore the differences and similarities between paranormal investigation and mediumship and to hopefully provide some helpful information those embarking on the Journey.

Chapter 1

IN THE BEGINNING...

"The eyes will see only what the mind is prepared to comprehend."
- Henri Bergson
French Philosopher

As with anything, you need to go back and blow the dust off the facts, events and people of the past. Traditionally, Americans struggle with history – I have no idea why. Perhaps because we have very little of our own compared to the rest of the world. But in this case, I think it bears reviewing what has transpired in the worlds of paranormal investigation and the birth of Spiritualism. Both sides of the aisle have gone through some significant evolution. And let me stress that there are battle lines drawn. I, of course, walked right into this battlefield, quite ignorant of both sides' intolerance for each other. More on that later. Let's look back and review.

> *par·a·nor·mal*/ˌperəˈnôrm(ə)l/**adjective**
> denoting events or phenomena such as telekinesis or clairvoyance that are beyond the scope of normal scientific understanding.

The term "paranormal" is a very general term. It was coined around 1915-1920 by nobody knows who. So many people have been credited with it or credited themselves for the term. Another tidbit lost in history. It is used to describe any phenomenon outside the range of normal experience and science's current ability to measure and understand. Under the paranormal umbrella you will find many things lumped together; ghost hunting, UFOs, Bigfoot/cryptozoology, voodoo and pretty much anything outside "non-specific bodies of knowledge".

Paranormal investigation is not a new process. The modern-day ghost hunter has no claim on inventing the process. It has been practiced throughout documented history. The earliest documented paranormal investigation was by Pliny the Younger of Ancient Greece. He pens a letter to Lucius Licinius Sura, a prominent Roman senator, and questions him on his views about "specters". He proceeds to describe two incidents in which "specters" were witnessed by different individuals. The first of the two mentioned involved a man named Curtius Rufus. He had traveled to Africa to visit the newly appointed governor and while walking down a very public square was visited by the apparition of a woman who prophesied future events in his life that were later documented as happening in his lifetime.

The second, more well-known occurrence documented by Pliny, the Greek philosopher was that of Athenodoros. Anthendoros was another Greek philosopher who came to Athens feeling the need to cloister himself to philosophize, I guess, and rents a villa for a pretty cheap price. I can't help but wonder just how much a philosopher made in 7 AD, but I'm thinking not too much. Thrilled with the bargain, he moves in. As he worked into the night, he was visited by an apparition of an aged, emaciated man dressed in rags and shackled in chains. He beckoned to Athenodoros to follow him into the courtyard of the villa. Upon arriving to a certain spot, he vanished. Athenodoros marks the spot and returns the next day, bringing the magistrate and some servants. He advises them to dig at the spot. There they find bones, mingled in with chains and rags. He orders the bones collected and properly buried. There were no further occurrences after the bones were cared for in a respectful manner. Hence, the first paranormal investigation. I love that story. It is by far the best haunting story ever.

In ancient cultures, there were individuals within communities who had the power and prestige to deal in the "spiritual" matters, such as shamans, medicine men, prophets and spiritual healers. All of these positions held the distinction of settling matters that involved the spirit realm. The history of the Oracles of Delphi is well documented; whatever way you choose to look at it. Are you able to see the dead after snorting methane gas? Maybe…With the advent of Christianity and other modern-day religions, these positions have been replaced by priests, ministers and rabbis.

In 1848 in Hydesville NY, the Fox Sisters burst onto the scene. **Maggie and Katie Fox** reported rappings in their Hydesville cottage. In order to communicate the girls fashioned a form of rappings representing the alphabet. It enabled the girls to determine they were communicating with the departed spirit of a peddler who was murdered and buried in the basement of the cottage. The word spread throughout their community, flooding the small cottage with people eager to witness the phenomenon. After finding human bones and a peddler's box buried under the house, the word of these events spread like wildfire, thus giving birth to the science and religion of today's modern Spiritualist

movement.

In the wake of this phenomenon, many self - proclaimed mediums cropped up over the world, but the highest concentration was in the US. It became a huge draw after the Civil War, as grieving mothers and widows clamored to the mediums to ease the grief of their loss of their sons and husbands. The Spiritualist newspaper, "The Banner of Light" was created in the 1860s to bring awareness to this new trend, to offer insight to the general population about the war effort, and also featured local mediums who attempted to connect families with their deceased soldiers.

Spiritualism became very fashionable across all social classes. Some historians insist that it was one of the first religions to become widespread through mass media. It was not uncommon for the wealthier classes to have its own medium on retainer. Invitations would be sent for "Tea & Table Tipping". These types of gatherings were becoming popular in the parlors of the elite. Séances were common events. At the height of the rage in the late 1880's, Spiritualism began to weaken due to accusations of fraud perpetrated by con artists. Compounding the issue was a very public statement by Katie Fox that the Hydesville rappings as well as the alleged mediumship communications with the dead were faked by herself and Maggie. Kate was paid $1500 by a reporter to publicly make the statement. Having fallen on hard times after many years of exploitation, she willingly did so. Maggie did not participate in the confession and continued to perform as a medium. Kate later tried to recant her statement, but the damage had already been done. Both sisters died in a poor economic state in their mid 50's.

Spiritualism has some high profile champions back in the day. Sir Arthur Conan Doyle is probably the most well-known. Doyle had lost a son to pneumonia after being wounded in WWI at the Battle of the Somme. He had a life-long interest in mystical subjects and the paranormal. He was initiated as a Freemason but later resigned. He was the founding member of the Hampshire Society for Psychical Research and later joined the

Society for Psychical Research in 1893.

He debated with many individuals that opposed his views, Harry Houdini for one. The two had a very public falling out regarding the Spiritualist process. Houdini was on a rampage exposing fraudulent mediums allegedly due to a less than satisfying reading from Doyle's wife, who attempted to communicate with Houdini's deceased mother (a touchy subject with Mssr. Houdini). Evidently this began the Houdini witch hunts to expose fraudulent mediums everywhere. I will not dwell on this for very long. It makes me sad. Sad, that fraudulent mediums always seem to crop up and give the authentic ones a bad name and, also sad, that pretty much it will always stay that way.

As these mediums were seemingly multiplying like kittens, the scientific community was getting its nose out of joint in a big way. Science was on a roll during this period. Parallel to this Spiritualist boom, there is a lot going on in science – Darwin presents his evolution concept, JJ Crookes invents the X-ray, Louis Pasteur develops the pasteurization process, Edison invents the stock ticker, Alfred Nobel invents dynamite (and they name a Peace Prize after him – go figure). The fact that so many people are embracing a concept that is deemed so non-scientific is not to be born! So, to remedy that, Harvard University puts together a crabby team of scientists that will travel the country investigating claims of the paranormal and debunk them. Period. If they are not able to debunk them, they are not to acknowledge the phenomenon. Objective research – right.

The literature of the day also contributed greatly to its popularity. Catherine Crowe (n'ee Stevens) was an English novelist and defender of women's rights who wrote gothic horror stories but tried to balance afterlife communication with some type of scientific research. She was heavily influenced by German research in this area, and her work "The Night Side of Nature" was said to be used as a base for the upcoming psychical research craze. She was, however, very critical of the scientific community declaring it was arrogant and presumptuous in stating all paranormal phenomena was the result of hysteria. She also felt most scientists "arranged the facts to their theory, not their theory to the facts". She laid down many ground rules for conducting paranormal research. She would get very little recognition for her contributions and lived out her life as a recluse until her death at age 86.

INVESTIGATORS OF THE PAST

In 1882, a conference was held in London to discuss the investigation and documentation of paranormal events and the formation of a group dedicated to conducting some type of formal research. The following month, Henry Sedgwick, Frederic Myers and Edmund Gurney and the British National Association of Spiritualists formed the Society for Psychical Research. Many well-known scientists and literary notables belonged to the group, including physicists Oliver Lodge and Michael Faraday and JJ Crookes. Samuel Clemens, Lewis Carroll, Alfred Lord Tennyson and Sir Arthur Conan Doyle also were members.

> *"The phenomenon is there, lying broadcast over the surface of history."*
> *- Williams James*
> *American author & psychologist*

Seeing the need to spread to America, the Society sought out Williams James who was an American philosopher and psychologist to head the Society. His views on investigating the paranormal were more objective and felt "most supernatural events were suspect" but felt science was remaining "deliberately blind". He was one of the founders of the American branch of SPR. The Society exists to this day and still does investigate paranormal claims.

> *My own mind is perfectly unprejudiced and impressible on the subject.*
> *I do not in the least pretend that such things are not. But ... I have not*
> *yet met with any Ghost Story that was proved to me, or that had not the noticeable*
> *peculiarity in it—that the alteration of some slight circumstance would*
> *bring it within the range of common natural probabilities.*
> *- Charles Dickens*
> *British author, social critic*

Not all individuals shared SPR's skeptical viewpoint about the paranormal. A small group of "convinced believers" began to meet quietly to discuss paranormal phenomena without the constraints of the Society for Psychical Research. Thus, the Ghost Club was born. The club has its roots in Cambridge and was launched officially in London in 1862. It included Charles Dickens, its founder, Sir Arthur

Conan Doyle and other literary bigwigs, such as Mark Twain, Lewis Carroll and

WB Yeats, are counted among its members. In this atmosphere, members were able to freely discuss varying viewpoints and theories without being subjected to the rigid perspectives of SPR. The group remained small and had some overlapping members with SPR. There was a short interval after Dickens death that the group discontinued meeting, but the club was eventually resurrected. They continue to meet to this day.

There are many individuals that can be credited to the beginnings of paranormal investigation. History is chocked full of characters that were at the heart of this wacky process.

One of the earliest investigators was **Harry Price (1881-1948)**. He was a prolific and talented writer and journalist, producing dozens of articles & several bestselling books. Mr. Price had his first paranormal experience while locked in an alleged "haunted house" at the age of 15 with a friend. With an interest in archaeology, magic and conjuring, he later became an amateur magician, thus having specific knowledge regarding sleight of hand techniques and illusions that were used by the fraudulent mediums. He was a member of SPR but was often at odds with them. Although he was well established in the annals of British psychical research, he was a controversial figure. Whispers of fraud and deception circled around some of his research, which is not unlikely when butting up against the opinion of the day. Unlike SPR and other contemporaries, he endorsed some mediums he felt to be genuine. He was a member of the Ghost Club and remained so until his death. He had built up a huge library of books, documents and case files relating to his career and the occult during his lifetime, which he bequeathed to the University of London.

Another forerunner in paranormal investigation was **George N.M. Tyrrell (1879-1952)**. He was an English physicist, mathematician and parapsychologist, but began as a student with the Marconi Foundation pioneering in developmental radio. He was one of the first investigators to introduce the topic of a supernatural nature into mainstream psychology. He joined the Society for Psychical Research in 1908, completely devoted himself to the subject. In 1945 he became president of the society. He published "The Personality of Man", but his book "Apparitions" is classified as actual theoretical study of psychical research. His classifications of apparitions is thought provoking and his system is still used today. He was also the first to introduce the term out-of-body experience. He proposed that ghosts were a hallucination of the unconscious and that collective experiences were a telepathic mechanism. He believed in telepathy, but was a stern critic of physical mediumship.

'I often wonder what the other side of the picture of haunting is in Ghost Land? Is it the dead alone that can disturb the living, or can the living similarly disturb the dead?"
- Nandor Fodor, Parapsychologist,
Author & Journalist

Another leader in the field would be Nandor Fodor (1895-1964). He was a British/American parapsychologist, psychoanalyst, author and journalist. He was a leading authority on poltergeists, hauntings and paranormal phenomena usually associated with mediumship. He pioneered the theory that poltergeists are external manifestations of conflicts within the subconscious rather than entities. In the 1930's, he was a correspondent for the Society for Paranormal Research and worked as an editor for the Psychoanalytic Review and was a member of the New York Academy of Science. His publications include the Encyclopedia of Psychic Sciences (1934). During this period, he embraced the paranormal, but then took an about face in the 1940's and advocated a psychoanalytical approach to psychic phenomena. He then began publishing skeptical newspaper articles on mediumship, which caused opposition from the Spiritualist community.

This is to be, by no means, an inclusive list but just the highlights. There are so many individuals who have contributed to this process. It would be impossible to touch on everyone.

RESEARCH AT A HIGHER LEVEL

What seems to be the root of the problem of the paranormal is the lack of true, serious and objective research. Science is evidently unable to remain objective – the academic community does present with some hope. There are universities with sanctioned paranormal research divisions. Some of the names may surprise you. Stanford University was the first academic institution in the US to study **ESP** and **psychokinetic energy**. Duke University developed a parapsychology lab as an offshoot of their psychology lab. In 1935, Duke researchers J.B. Rhine and William McDougall became the second institution in the country to establish a program after a lecture by Arthur Conan Doyle. To this day, Rhine is regarded as the father of parapsychology. The Rhine name is no longer associated with Duke but now lives on with the Rhine Research Center where research continues into the phenomenon of ESP and PK energy.

As these two programs have been discontinued, a couple of institutions have managed to keep their programs afloat. The University of Virginia developed a Division of Perceptual Studies in 1967. It has explored such phenomena as reincarnation (most specifically through its focus on children who claim to remember past lives), **near death experiences (NDEs)**, apparitions and after-death communications, altered states of consciousness, as well as many other psychic (psi) experiences. The Division credits its persistence over time with the great success it has had in substantiating claims within its reincarnation research.

The University of Arizona is another institution that has developed a good program over time. The VERITAS program was established in 2006 and continued for a couple years. Its focus was survival after death and mediumship. In 2008, it reinvented its program to SOPHIA and broadened their research to include angels, divine power and spirit guides. Across the pond, the University of Edinburgh in Scotland developed the Koestler Parapsychology Unit within their Psychology Department. Their main focus is ESP and psychokinesis. They have managed to bring research into the 21st century by conducting mass research projects in the areas of ESP and **remote viewing**. Other notable institutions are the University of Adelaide in Australia, Lund University in Sweden and the University of London, Goldsmith in England.

Whereas these institutions should be commended for opening the door for serious research on some topics of psychic phenomenon, the ghost issue continues to remain on the fringe.

THE MODERN GHOST HUNTER

In the early 1990s, paranormal research took a real scientific bend and attempted to take paranormal investigation further down a more concrete path. Research was pursued regarding energy manipulation, electromagnetic field disturbance and how it relates to the paranormal. In the entertainment field, paranormal investigation has risen to a fever pitch. Television has jumped on that bandwagon and provides us with more ghost hunting shows as there is air time.

> *"A ghost hunter without a medium is like an angler without a fish"*
> *- Hans Holzer*
> *Paranormal Investigation Pioneer*

One of the most high-profile investigator and foremost authority on the subject was/is **Hans Holzer (1920-2009)**. He was born in Austria and earned his PhD in History and Anthropology. He taught Psychology at New York Institute of Technology. Holzer was open to any and all forms of evidence gathering when it came to paranormal investigation. Ghosts, according to Holzer, imprints left on the environment. He felt spirits were intelligent beings who could interact with the living and "stay-behinds" were those who found themselves earthbound after death. Holzer routinely worked with such mediums as Marisa Anderson and Ethel Johnson-Meyers as well as a British witch named Sybil Leek. This did not make him popular with the scientific "debunker" community, but he could have cared less. SPR was openly critical of

Holzer who endorsed the mediums who worked with him. He carried on with his lifelong research without the dogma imposed upon the field by so-called scientific investigators. His most famous case was the Amityville Horror house. He remains to this day, the foremost authority on the subject, authoring more than 120 books on the subject. His daughter is attempting to keep his work in the forefront by releasing private files on some of his more sensational cases to be presented on TV. The exciting thing about this, at least for me, is hearing snippets of Ethel Myers during her channeling sessions in these locations.

I'm very hands-on. I was very hands-on with talking to individuals. That's very important, whether it be someone giving me advice or trying to find out some type of information. If I have additional questions, I always get behind-the-scenes and dig in and talk to individuals.
- John Zaffis
Paranormal Investigator & Demonologist

John Zaffis (1955 -) has a long and rich history in the field of paranormal investigation. His journey started as a young man learning the paranormal at the knee of his aunt and uncle, Ed and Lorraine Warren, of the Amityville Horror fame. The Warrens worked together on several cases involving hauntings and possessions all over the United States. Ed was a retired law enforcement officer as well as a self-professed, self-trained demonologist, author and lecturer. Lorraine was a clairvoyant and light trance medium who worked closely with Ed. Both were very influential to Zaffis early in his career. He has appeared in numerous paranormal TV shows as well as his own show, Haunted Collector. He runs the Paranormal and Demonology Research Society of New England as well as functions as curator for the Museum of the Paranormal that is in Strathford Connecticut. He has studied the works of Roman Catholic priests, monks, Buddhists, rabbis, and ministers that are prominent exorcists in the field. Zaffis lectures at events, universities across the country. His 41 years in the field has taken him worldwide on his quest.

"If your cat is speaking Latin, you could have a problem."
- Jason Hawes, Founder, TAPS

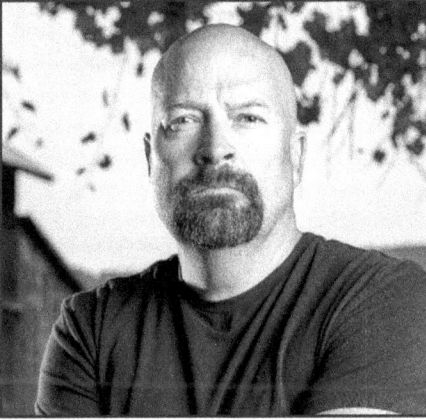

We would also have to tip the hat to the ghost hunters that visit us on the air waves, starting with TAPS, The Atlantic Paranormal Society. Founded by **Jason Hawes (1971 -)** in 1990, it enjoyed many years on TV and certainly has a rabid following. They can be credited in influencing the start of many amateur ghost groups, including two I have been associated with. Early on in my exploration into the paranormal, I had the opportunity to see TAPS at the Lily Dale Assembly during the summer program. I saw the word "ghost" in the program and handed over the money. At the beginning of the presentation, Jason Hawes jokingly asked who had heard of them – my arm was the only one not up. I realized at that point I was a bit behind on the ghost issue. They were the main group that approached paranormal investigation solely from a scientific standpoint and dismisses any psychic/mediumship input.

These days anyone can hang out a shingle and claim they are a paranormal investigator (much like the mediums of old). There is certainly no shortage of airtime on the small screen regarding the paranormal. I will not debate the issue of who is or is not qualified. Any research is welcome. What I don't welcome is some of the networks that are plying the public with sensationalism. Well, that sounds familiar…fraudulent mediums at the turn of the century plying the public with supernatural claims…and now, TV executives at the turn of the next century, plying the public with exaggerated claims of the paranormal. You know what they say about glass houses…

Chapter 2

WHAT ARE WE HUNTING?

"Paranormal investigation is the 21st century's answer to the séance."
Author Unknown

The thing about both paranormal investigation and the world of the medium is that there is so much overlap that is not being acknowledged by either side. I feel it is important to realize we are both working toward the same goal but taking different paths to get there. There may be some differences in opinion, but that is a good thing. Having these differences of opinions is what makes a good team a great team. Following dogma blindly does not give good research data. I have been fortunate to be associated with a few great teams of investigators. Billy is the head of the last team I worked with. We met each other as members of a previous team. He was very up front with me from the beginning stating, "...he really was not sure he was on board with what I do". I was cool with that. Too many groups on both sides of the aisle are prone to being blind followers, not be able to analyze an issue or phenomenon objectively. What is important is to give respect to each other for what is brought to the table.

To continue here, we need to sort out what we are hunting. For the sake of neutrality, let us look at paranormal issues by phenomena. We will explore them, hopefully with some degree of objectivity.

"When people tell me they don't believe in ghosts and spirit forces,
what they are really saying is that they are not familiar with the data."
- Ed Warren
American Paranormal Investigator & Demonologist

Let us look at the data – a 2009 CBS poll reported that 48% of Americans believe in ghosts without ever having an experience, while other surveys have shown that roughly one-third of people polled believe in haunted houses. That, in my opinion is a large number, but when looking at the history, the concept has been around forever. All cultures and religions have some form of a perceived "spirit" or "ghost".

Most religions teach that the spiritual aspect of human beings, whether it is called a soul or spirit, survives beyond the Transition called Death. Is it possible for that soul or spirit to linger on the physical plane and not make a full transition? If so, these entities would be classified as ghosts. Merriam Webster defines it as such:

GHOST: n.\ *disembodied soul; esp: the soul of a dead person believed to inhabit an unseen world or to appear in bodily form to living people.*

They have many names, such as earthbound spirits, disincarnate energy, grounded spirit, wraith, haint, poltergeist, shade, shadow, specter, ghast - this list is endless. If you delve into cultural backgrounds, it becomes even more fascinating. The historical record can give us many different concepts.

Greece is well represented regarding spirits in the literature of the time. Don't forget our friend Athendoros from the introduction. He is our Scooby Doo of the ancient world. Homer used the term "psyche" to describe spirits. Skia is also a term from classical Greek that translates into "shadow". Souls were not expected to return, but sometimes did. Picture it: you are hanging out in your lovely villa staring off into the Mediterranean and POP! You see an apparition of your long dead great auntie. What to do? Your first step in resolving this issue would be a visit to one of the Oracles of Delphi. She could intervene to determine the problem. If the issue was severe, it may involve hiring a psychagogia. The term translates to "soul leading". This individual was a spirit raiser – a specialist in raising spirits as well as quieting them. Sometimes a sacrifice was necessary to summon the ghost to have a conversation as to why they are angry or to identify their issue. I am sure there was always some type of fee to put them at rest – capitalism in its infancy.

Ancient Rome also references a co-existence with the afterlife. Unfortunately, with the Romans, it is hard to distinguish between what was actual documentation and what was fiction. Pliny the Elder (not to be confused with Pliny the Younger, again from our introduction), was a Roman author, a naturalist, philosopher, and a naval and army commander of the early Roman Empire. He wrote extensively on this subject. It is eluded that he was a bit of a prevaricator and give to wild exaggerations, along with other writers and statesmen of the time, so the documented history of this time is subject as to the level of its authenticity.

Roman literature was filled with many strange entities (centaurs, tall spirit women, ghostly apparitions). The term Manes or DiManes is thought to refer to members of the natural band of dead ancestors and close relatives. They were viewed to function as guiding and protective force in daily Roman life. There was a nine-day festival called Parentalia that was held in February in their honor. Roman tombstones often bore two letters: DM, short for dis manibus – 'To the spirits of the departed'. This has been interpreted to be a calling card to the afterlife alerting them that another spirit was on its way and needed to be greeted and escorted to their next level of existence.

Lemurs were in fact grotesque skeletal specters who would wander the earth at night causing hurt and injury to the living. They were thought to be the unrest souls of thieves and criminals, the executed and the damned, or for whatever other reason they had not been given a proper funeral. The Roman poet Ovoid described them as "voiceless spirits" who would walk the earth, terrifying all those who crossed their paths as they wandered the streets at night. An early springtime festival known as Lemuria was held to keep these undesirable spirits at bay.

The First People from the Cherokee tribe in America have the Raven Mocker as other tribes also have some sort of ghost legend/stories about various scary beings. Burial rituals were essential to keep the dead at rest. "Ghost Sickness" was recognized as a preoccupation or possession by the dead. This was viewed as part of the grieving process with symptoms of weakness, loss of appetite, recurring nightmares. A ritual was performed by tribal members to expel the offending spirit. The Shoshoni tribe recognized Whirlwinds that were thought to be apparitions. The Chindi (Navajo) felt these apparitions were the leftover collection of negative energy from someone who died violently. It seemed that all tribes specifically believed in good and evil spirits and felt evil spirits were necessary to keep the balance.

The Transition Called Death

> *"Death is no more than passing from one room to the next."*
> *- Helen Keller*
> *American Author & Political Activist*

As we embark on this discussion regarding ghosts, it is important to talk about what happens at the time of the transition called death. The following description is a compilation of many different areas and information sources. I have tried to leave out any religious undertones, not because I believe they do not exist, but just to give an objective description of what I believe happens.

It has been reported by individuals who are present at the passing of a person's passing, such as hospice workers and nurses, that the person in transition reacts to many different stimuli they seem to be visualizing or experiencing. They report calling out to long deceased relatives or seem to be undergoing some type of transformation. The person is shedding their physical body to be able to pass into their next plane of existence. In Spiritualist circles as well as other religions, there occurs a detachment of what is referred to as the **Silver Cord**. This cord is kind of like an umbilical cord that tethers the physical body to the **etheric body (body double)**. It acts as a lifeline to the physical world. Once the cord is severed, the transition called death occurs.

Experiences can differ from person to person, as described by many experiencing **near death experiences (NDE)**. It may be affected by opinions, beliefs, and attitudes we acquire during life. Some individuals reported being greeted by deceased loved ones and friends, spirit guides and angels. Others see deities, such as Jesus, Mohammed and the Buddha. There are even reports of seeing deceased pets that were a big part of their lives in the physical world. There is a theory that individuals who undergo a long, drawn out, debilitating illness or are in a comatose/altered state of consciousness will tend to drift in and out of their physical body until they finally make a full transition. I have experienced communication from individuals like this while giving readings, although it was only a couple of instances, but I found it very interesting.

Here is where things become fractured. Religious beliefs will bend the experience to fit into their specific dogma. The bottom line is that no one really knows what lies beyond. At this point, the concept of a **discarnate energy** comes into play. How does one reject the idea of a full transition and remain close to the physical plane? Are we able to exercise free will and reject any guiding forces and remain on the lower levels of the astral plane? There are theories abound, both from a religious and scientific standpoint. Both seem to be firmly rooted on who is right and who is wrong. All parties must be willing to entertain all possibilities in order to produce good, solid evidence to the Truth..

TYPES OF GHOSTS

"There are an infinite number of universes existing side by side and
through which our consciousness's constantly pass.
In these universes, all possibilities exist. You are alive in some,
long dead in others, and never existed in still others.
Many of our "ghosts" could indeed be visions of people going
about their business in a parallel universe or another time – or both."

- Paul F. Eno
American Paranormal Investigator & Journalist

So, in the modern world, what is the difference between a spirit and a ghost? In my world, I try to break it down to a simple definition; ghosts are deceased individuals, who have either decided to stay grounded on this plane of existence or remain close to the earth plane for a specific reason after the transition of death. Spirits are entities who have made the full transition to their next plane of existence and may come back in visitation to the earth plane for any manner of reasons to communicate with the living. Our focus right now is on the ghost.

I am not out to write War & Peace on this topic. This is by no means an exhaustive list, but I felt that if the reader wished to examine one of these phenomena further, this will serve as a jumping off point. Many may have other phenomena they feel should be considered, but these are the highlights:

Type	Description
Intelligent	- Was once human - Is aware of their surroundings and can react and interact with the living world - Usually seeking acknowledgment and/or assistance - Some respond to requests to make themselves known - My own slant on this phenomenon is that an entity that is grounded to a specific location, or who hangs close to the physical plane and rejects the opportunity to progress to their next plane of existence, is a ghost. • There are times I feel that there is phenomenon that is caused by a spirit who has crossed to their next plane of existence but comes back in visitation for a specific purpose or has a message for the living.

Type	Description

Residual Energy	- Activity or recurring event from the past that leaves an imprint on the environment
	"Stone tape theory"
	- No spirit energy – just trapped energy
	    • Energy is stored magnetically in the environment. Over time energy levels builds and discharges showing a "replay" of the event
	    • Is thought to dissipate over time
	- Can be held in non-biological inanimate objects
	- Cannot interact or communicate with the living
	- This would include inanimate ghosts such as the Flying Dutchman and phantom trains and cars. They repeat their final moments over and over
	- Anniversary hauntings may fall under this category
	    • The disturbance may fall at or during the date of the imprint or disaster

Inhuman	An entity that did not begin their existence in physical form Demonic haunting or possession and can encompass many different phenomena at once:
	    • Auditory sounds such a growls, screeches, voices that seem to speak gibberish, etc.
	    • Smells (putrid odors, sulfur)
	    • Infestation of insects (i.e. flies)
	- Elementals or nature spirits that are said to predate mankind
	    • Represents the elements of earth, air, fire and water, each having their own elemental.
	    • These are ancient energies that never walked in bodily form.
	    • Said to cause phenomenon, but not necessarily with intent to harm – not good or bad, they just are.

Type	Description
Poltergeist	- German for "noisy ghost" – is it really a ghost? - RSPK – residual spontaneous psychokinesis - Said to be generated by the unconscious mind - Can be triggered by a traumatic situation or a time of great stress usually centered around one person (agent) • Has been linked to onset of puberty

Below are other types of phenomenon that did not easily fit into the above categories, but are worth mentioning:

Type	Description
Crisis apparition	- Viewing an apparition of an individual in times of great stress - Often reported seeing someone at the time of their death sometimes referred to as a "death bed apparition" - Can be someone that has a have a strong emotional connection to the apparition
Shadow people	Differences of opinion on this phenomena. Are they: - Low level entities – "bottom feeders" or, - Lack of an energy source to assist in manifestation or, - May indicate the entity's level of spiritual development or, - Entities that infringe on our timeline/dimension • Time travelers • Inter-dimensional beings - For some reason, they most always seem like they are wearing some type of head gear (i.e. hat, hood, cloak, etc. I always wondered what was up with that)
Animal ghosts	- Cherished animal family members who have passed - May be a guide or totem animal making itself known - Can be associated with a haunting • Bell Witch haunting had reports of phantom birds and dogs in the area during the time of the haunting episodes (see portal hauntings)

Type	Description

Doppelganger

- A German loan word used in the 1800's meaning "double doer"or "double walker"
- Is seen as a non-biologically related look-alike or double of a living person, sometimes portrayed as a ghostly paranormal phenomenon and traditionally seen as a harbinger of bad luck
- "Phantom forerunner" may fall into this category
  - Projection of a living person arriving at a location before the actual physical body
- Previously this phenomenon was referred to as a fetch
- There are many examples of this phenomenon down through history in a variety of cultures:
  - Ancient Egypt called it "ka" that translates to "spirit double"
  - In Norse mythology, a vardøger is a ghostly double who is seen performing the person's actions in advance. This gave way to a greeting in Norway "…is that you or your vardøger ?"
  - There are other examples in many different cultures down throughout history, all with the same back story.

Artificial Ghost

- This is actually a "conjured ghost"
- Capacity to create and sustain an image that can be empowered with a life of its own
- Can be found in many cultures
  - Tulas – Tibetean
  - Golem – Jewish magical tradition
- Thought to be a manifestation of the collective unconscious
- One incident was documented in the book "Conjuring Phillip: An Adventure in Psychokinesis
  - Investigated by the Toronto Society for Psychical Research
  - He was given a complete name, history of likes, dislikes and even a tragic ending by suicide
  - Could communicate with this entity during a séance with -raps and knocks

Type	Description
Artificial Ghost (cont.)	- Another incident is contributed by Alexandra David Neel (1868-1969) • French mystic and adventurer and the first female lama and only outsider to be indoctrinated into secret Tibetan doctrine • Shut herself into a meditative stated and "formed" a monk- short, chubby and jolly • He appeared and disappeared at will, but eventually turned surly. Others began to see him as well, so felt it was time to end his existence

Back to our original question: "Why are you here?". The list seems endless and very personal and unique to each entity:

• Some may have issues with people, family and things on the physical level they are not willing to give up (alcohol or drug addictions, sex, food, etc.)
• Fear of retribution for their actions in the physical world
• A perception that they may not wish to see someone undesirable (an abusive spouse, someone that harmed them in the physical world)
• Some may have a sense of responsibility to the living (i.e. children, spouse left behind) and choose to stay close to the earth plane
• Physical additions
• Revenge – inability to find forgiveness for an injury done to them in the physical world
• Sudden death (i.e. murder, suicide, accident, unexpected medical condition)
• Lack of understanding of what the afterlife is all about

I put child spirits into this last category. I was always under the impression someone was always waiting there to meet and guide transitioning spirits, certainly and most definitely children. I posed the idea to my mentor, Judith who replied, "…well, they can be very fast.", which I interpreted as feeling that freedom and immediately are off! Additionally, she commented they will have a tendency to flock up and run in packs as transient spirits, going from place to place.

Past team members Bill and Katie have six kids between them. When the kids were small, their house was a chaotic and loving place with a big yard, lots of bunk beds, toys, complete with chickens and goats in the back yard. They both have seen little ones here and there. Katie has been wakened in the night by the sound of someone calling "Mama". She thought it was one of her kids but upon investigating, all were asleep. She was at a loss to what or who it was. I smiled – who wouldn't want to live there? They both emit a loving, accepting energy that I am sure any child spirit would home in on and try to be part of their tribe.

OTHER TYPES OF PHENOMENON

"I shall not commit the fashionable stupidity of regarding everything I cannot explain as a fraud."

C.J. Jung
Swiss psychiatrist and psychoanalyst

Portals & Vortexes

These two phenomena are frequently used interchangeably. They are two separate phenomena but seem to have a symbiotic relationship. Portals are classified as an opening or gateway to, well you name it. It could be the afterlife, another dimension, another time. No one really knows. What is hypothesized is that spirits and entities can use this opening as a doorway into this plane of existence. It is described as a region of space that has a four dimensional vibratory frequency where the three and four dimensions merge. Out of the ordinary phenomenon is reported in these places, and not just paranormal manifestations.

Some of those places are the Skinwalker Ranch in Utah, San Luis in Colorado and the Bridgewater Triangle in Massachusetts. There can be audible noises and buzzing and items may be found around the area, such as apports (items that appear that are not usually found in the area).

If captured on film they can appear to be rope-like, opaque and can reflect colors. This photo was taken on a whim to capture the front of this private residence in Lilydale NY, and the result was the capture of a potential portal.

Vortexes exist in places with a strong gravitational anomaly and creates a spiral pull of energy. It is said to be more common at the convergence of earth's ley lines. Some examples would be Sedona Arizona in the US, Glastonbury in Somerset England and Stonehenge. Vortexes are what gives portals the energy to open and develop. It is almost like the portal is the car and the vortex is the gas. The vortex provides the energy or the spiral pull that can create the portal. This energy may provide assistance to spirits to manifest in a more distinct form. The energy that is emitted from these vortexes can be either positive or negative. Feelings that one would experience around this type of opening would determine what type of energy it is. One theory describes the vortexes as inflow or outflow. An inflow vortex has energy flowing into the earth. This energy will feel heavier and more negative emotions like fear and anger may be experienced. Outward flow vortexes have energy flowing out of the earth and are generally uplifting and revitalizing. Folks who have experienced Sedona Arizona can attest to the uplifting feeling one experiences there. Highly sensitive people can experience a wide range of emotions and feelings around these places.

There are multiple sources out on the internet (use caution as always) but it is always good to expose yourself to all opinions and theories. The site Vortex Hunters provides a map of vortexes by state and also by country. It will also give history of phenomenon at these sites.

Thought-Forms

I found this concept quite thought provoking. I felt that I wanted to devote a little time to this idea. A **thought-form** is defined as a nonphysical entity or object created by thought that exists in the mental or astral plane. In 1901, CW Leadbeater and Annie Besant, two gifted clairvoyants at the turn of the last century, wrote a book on thought forms. They classified "thoughts as things" that can manifest into the physical. They can radiate out and attract "like energies" as stated in the **Law of Attraction**, which could manifest on the physical plane. They can be both negative and positive, as all things are in nature. These forms build up in a person's energy field or aura, creating and influencing behavior and characteristics.

The lifespan and endurance of a thought-form depends on the nature and intensity of the thought. Most thought forms are benign and will dissipate over time. Some with great intensity can become anchored on the astral and/or the physical plane. They exist as long as they are energized by collective thought. When they fade from interest, they return to formlessness on the astral plane.

Negative thoughts weaken a person and can even facilitate the onset of illness. They can be caused by trauma, emotional upheaval or are our "baggage" we carry with us and are not able to resolve. Thoughts that are low in nature, such as anger, hate, lust, and greed, create thought-forms that are on a lower development level. Thoughts of a more spiritual nature generate forms that have greater purity, clarity, and refinement and can act as a protective, energizing shield. Again, we have the duality of positive and negative.

Does this somehow explain the "mob mentality"? When a group of like-minded individuals congregate, be it positive or negative, can these thought forms develop and **manifest** themselves into the environment? Do some individuals possess the ability to take those forms and place them into the collective unconscious? That would explain much about times in history where the negative was overwhelmingly used to manipulate the masses, such as Nazi Germany, the cult following of Jonestown, and on a smaller scale, the Charles Manson cult group, Waco, Heaven's Gate and others. Can this also explain the rise of the negativity of groups of Neo Nazis and white supremacy groups in present day?

On the other hand, positive thoughts can have a beneficial effect on ourselves and our environment. Look at the magic that was created at Woodstock or Martin Luther King's march on Washington. Removing any opinion that you may have connected to either example, they were extraordinary events that generated positive energy,

As mediums and investigators, the places we go to investigate, such as old prisons, jails, asylums and hospitals are usually brimming with negativity, sorrow, regret and anger. Are these thought forms we are seeing on video or hearing on audio? Again, when we investigate a private residence and there has been significant trauma or violence on the premises, are the residual thought forms causing the phenomenon the residents are calling a haunting? Good investigators will take copious notes what they observe in the environment and issues and events that are present in their client's lives. It is sobering to think that our thoughts can have that much power.

Soul Fragments/Fragmentation

There are many different perspectives on this subject, and I hesitated to include it here, but I think this needs to be put out there for consideration. Soul fragments/fragmentation are parts of the soul/psyche that are lost or rejected by the Self to bury unpleasant memories or trauma. Our unconscious mind is a powerful thing. It will reject or move away from painful situations and traumatic events in our lives and will leave a hole or gap in the unconscious. When we experience trauma, part of our soul or spirit separates from us in order to not feel the full impact of trauma. Theoretically, when these fragments try to reconnect with the Source, a person may feel uncomfortable and uneasy, liking to a feeling of an attachment or possession. Furthermore, there is another theory that these fragmented areas may be used by transient entities to gain access to an individual, again resulting in a type of possession/obsession situation. Some symptoms of this fragmentation may be recurring dreams, loss of interest and/or creativity, feeling disconnected, lack of motivation, high anxiety just to name a few.

I can't help but wonder if these fragmented pieces of a person's Self can manifest itself while trying to reconnect with its Source. It may be a something to consider when running across a client who has suffered a loss or trauma, or if a client reports an uneasy or jittery feeling of a paranormal nature. It would be advisable to have the affected person seek out an energy worker that can assist with reconnecting broken parts to their Home.

Attachments/Possession

Both of these topics have some sort of overlap or similarity to each other, which makes comparing them difficult. This is another area that has more sides to it than a prism. Immediately upon uttering the words, something dark and evil will come to mind. Hollywood has done a great job of scaring the crap out of us all, with movies depicting snarling, growling, the spinning of heads and regurgitation of pea soup. There are plenty of opinions on these subjects, but we will touch on each of them in turn.

I have run across what I perceived as an attachment situation a few times. There is a distinct possibility that this may present itself during an investigation. It would be prudent to add a few questions about behavior changes with anyone in the structure that is to be investigated, be it a home or place of business that could be related to recent deaths of family members or individuals who are close to the client. People clump the terms attachment and possession as one in the same, but I feel there is a distinct difference between the two.

Traditionally, an attachment refers to a soul who has passes from the earth plane and attaches their energy to that of a living person for the purpose of using their energy or to manipulate their actions for their own motives while the host maintains their own personality. Grounded spirits are challenged when it comes to an energy source. They do not have access to the Light, either from being in a confused state or they reject the Light for one reason or another as we previously discussed. They have limited access to an energy source. They can leech energy from natural sources such as running water, geomagnetic fields, and some feel solar flares can ramp up paranormal action and can be an energy source, but the living is the most powerful, reliable source.

Attachments may show themselves slowly, Changes in the host become noticeable because it is almost like the host's personality is being pushed aside by the attaching spirit. They may take on new and different personality traits. The host may experience a few symptoms, as listed here.

Signs and Symptoms of a Spirit Attachment
- Lethargy and feeling exhausted
- Sudden onset of irritability, crankiness, or snappiness
- Anger or rage issues not previously present
- Drug or Alcohol Dependence (either new or a recurrence)
- Extreme and often dangerous mood fluctuations
- Any sudden behavioral or personality change
- A feeling of heaviness or pressure
- Waking up to presences around you at night
- Feeling like being "dragging" or weighed down on a frequent basis
- Developing new vices
- Negative outlook on life not previously present
- Pain in specific areas of the body that has seemingly no other cause
- Bizarre, haunting, and horrifying dreams

This can evolve into a type of symbiotic relationship. The two are sharing energy, and that will begin to take a toll on the living host. Some compare it to being pregnant.

There are lots of theories and ideas of how and why this can happen. We already realize that grounded spirits have issues. They have a strong bond with the physical plane for one reason or another and are drawn to resonating energy. There is a strong drive to still be connected to the living. In the **Universal Law of Attraction**, like attracts like. If the host already has a pre-existing issue that resonates with the deceased, it can be magnified. Entities who perhaps were abusers of alcohol or drugs, tobacco and other vices may connect with a living host that enjoys the same thing. Most do not intentionally mean any harm, but to a recovering addict, be it drugs, alcohol, sex, food or whatever, the pull can be very strong. Eventually, this sharing of energy can and will take a toll.

Interestingly, if the host can resolve the shared issue and come to terms with their addictive behavior, the attachment will have nothing in common with their host. This time is ideal to help in moving them to their next plane of existence. There are some sources that feel that nothing can come in or out of your energy without your permission. Over 90% of our behavior is governed by the Unconscious. There needs to be a strong sense of Self to reject this connection.

There are a few well known practitioners in psychotherapy circles that deal with this phenomenon. **Dr. Edith Fiore** (1930 -) is a psychotherapist who was trained in an orthodox manner but developed an opinion regarding attachments/possession during her research. She performed many de-possessions through her techniques. They are well documented in her book "The Unquiet Dead" where she presents case studies of her journey in moving them on to their next plane of existence.

William Baldwin (1930 -) is another in the field of psychotherapy that does similar work to Fiore. He carries out counseling sessions with both the human and spirit to resolve their issues. It is a fine line to determine whether an individual is suffering from this type of phenomenon or have a mental health issue on your hands.

Possession, on the other hand, seems to have levels of intensity and depending on who you speak with, may or may not exist at all. There are some "possessions" or "impressions" (possession lite) that are benign. Some entities that are not fully disconnected with the earth plane may influence the living. Can departed souls who have strong ties to a living person influence their behavior? This is something that investigators need to discuss with clients during a pre-investigative screening. If someone in the household has had a change in behavior or personality, this may be a possibility. Some in the psychological community would call this a grief reaction; an individual taking on the personality traits of a deceased loved one or chalking it up to a split personality disorder or dissociative identity disorder. All depends upon your point of view, doesn't it?

If you ask a medium, particularly a trance medium (of which there are very few these days) the difference between possession and channeling they would probably respond with "not much". Channeling can be viewed as a form of temporary possession, but with this process the medium is giving permission for discarnate energies to communicate with the living through them. Possession, on the other hand, is said to take place without the consent of the host. Believe it or not, it can be benign in nature but it is never a good thing in the long run.

In 1877 there was a woman named Mary Lurancy who lived in Watseka, IL. One day she suffered from convulsions and went into a trance-like state for hours. She then developed multiple personalities that began speaking through her. She then reported to see spirits around her and channeled them. After a while, one of the dominant spirits announced all they spirits she had been channeling were departing for the spirit world and would allow Mary to resume her own life. Is this possession or obsession or a personality disorder?

Historically, demonic possession is a phenomenon that is based in Christianity but is shared in various degrees with other faiths and cultures as well. In the 1960's anthropologist Erika Bourguignon conducted a study of possession in 488 societies. Seventy four percent of them maintained some belief in spirit possession. Spiritualists do not subscribe to this concept, feeling that there are only higher and lower order spirits. In fact, they will not use the word possession at all. I am firmly planted on the fence on this one. Being of a Spiritualist bend, I do recognize the existence of higher and lower spirits; ones who are more evolved and exist on the higher planes. Where things become murky for me is the religious aspect of the phenomenon. Who is to say that the Christian rite of exorcism will solve this issue when Islam, Judaism, and Buddhism also have some version of this in their belief system. Who's to say your "demon" is Christian or Muslim or Jew? I certainly would have a time sorting that one out. A lot may depend on the individual who is having the issue and what their belief system would be. At any rate, it is good to know when to draw the line and know when the situation is over the heads of the investigator and the medium, and to defer to either a mental health professional or a religious counselor that can assist the individual in question.

As a side note, there is a phenomenon that cannot be technically classified as a possession but certainly has the hallmark of one. **Walk-Ins** are defined as a person whose original soul departs the body and is replace by a departed soul. This type of soul swap can happen during times of extreme trauma such as accidents, illness, during operative procedures and near death experiences. Many spouses will say the individual's personality is greatly altered and are barely recognizable as the same person before the event. It would be reasonable to assume that a life change would not be out of the ordinary, however this change goes much deeper.

Yet again, our friends in Hollywood have represented this happening in movies and television. The 1941 movie "Here Comes Mr. Jordan" and "Heaven Can Wait" (both the original and the 1978 remake) are examples. Television's "X-Files" and "Ghost Whisperer" are other examples from the little screen.

Some of these occurrences are thought to be a mutual consent with a living soul and a departed soul to either complete some sort of task or mission that was not completed during their lifetime. In this way, the task could be completed faster without waiting for **reincarnation**. Others are wandering spirits looking for a second chance at life, be it a selfish motive or seeks to complete a task left undone in their lifetime. There is even a concept that a blend of many souls or essences can inhabit one body. Medically, this may be classified as some type of multiple personality disorder, but who knows? Think of how many individuals who claimed mediumship capabilities in the past and were institutionalized and medicated. It is only now being marginally more socially accepted as a "gift" rather than being branded a lunatic.

There is not a lot of references written on the subject because of its controversial nature, but I felt it was worth mentioning.

Orbs

This topic has to be one of the most hotly debated issues in the paranormal world. Again, the width of division between the sides are as wide as the Grand Canyon. Either an orb is nothing (bug, dust, lens flair, etc.) or every single thing that ends up on the camera lens is an orb. Let's build a bridge.

A good description I found is from Amanda Lynette Meeder who states orbs are a concentration of energy (electrical, electrons, particles of matter) that is dense enough to produce a reflection. It can depend on the environment as in weather, humidity and the like and also the media in which it was captured. It would seem like a plausible explanation as to how they appear frequently under the IR and /or night vision. Video and film seem to do a good job of it but can cast doubt as well as confirmation. I have, however spoken to many individuals who have seen them with their naked eye.

Meeder hypothesizes that the presence of orbs is a concentration of energy that is created by a high vibrational spirit, as in spirits who have made a full transition, spirit guides and angelic presences, not earthbound entities. Spirits who have not

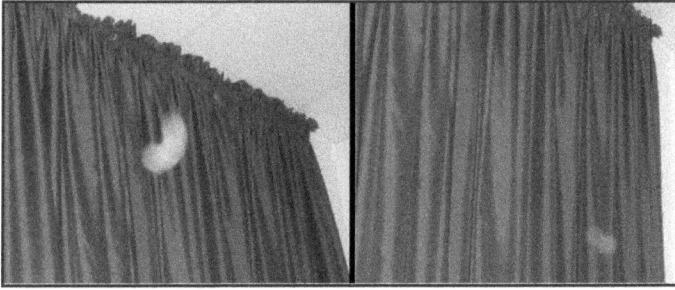

made that full transition are in a constant search for energy sources, hence the washed out look of a reported apparition or seeing shadow forms. If the entity is low on fuel, it cannot project very clearly

This picture was taken in total darkness by my friend Anita during one of our frequent stays in Lilydale. She stated she was compelled to point the camera in a certain direction and shoot, which she did. What a capture! We affectionately dubbed it the "Macaroni Orb" as it's shape in the first picture resembles elbow macaroni.

I have found other hypotheses that orbs can sometimes be earthbound spirits and seem to require the least amount of energy in order to manifest. There also may be a correlation between orbs and a high amount of EMF which may appear in photos and videos as an orb.

There are dozens of theories out there that will explain it away. One of my favorites is ball lightning. Very little is known about this phenomenon due to it being such a rare event, but seeing what little documentation is out there, I can't imagine someone mistaking this for an orb. As mentioned before, the standard "dust, bug, water particles, etc." theories are always in the forefront. I also find that digital cameras can pull off some very strange looking things depending on lighting and shutter speed. The investigators who opt for film capture and the old fashioned Polaroid route may have a point. At any rate, it is advised to be objective when analyzing this piece of evidence. As a medium, take into account what you were feeling and sensing at the time of the capture. Your intuition will tell you if a presence is there or not. Other evidence should be considered to see if it makes a correlation.

Haunted Places

"Now about those ghosts. I'm sure they are here and I'm not half so alarmed at meeting them as I am having to meet the live nuts I have to see every day."
- Bess Truman
Former First Lady

What makes a house haunted? Is it the presence of a disembodied spirit or the left behind residual energy of some past trauma or tragedy? Is it a portal that serves as a superhighway to the afterlife? All of this can contribute to a place having activity. **Haunted places** are a paranormal investigator's bread and butter. We all are clamoring for a chance to investigate at the big paranormal meccas. Many old buildings or historic sites claim a good portion of activity, but what fuels it? What makes it present itself? There are tons of questions associated with this phenomenon. Some places may lie dormant for years but then awakes by some action or event. The most common reason that is used relentlessly by the paranormal community is the remodel. Dick and Jane buy an old turn of the century Victorian. They are anxious to get the hardwoods refinished, new windows, and the new furnace installed. In the middle of everything, workmen start to report lost and/or moved tools, bangs and clanks are heard at all hours of the day and night and as the climax, the report of an apparition on the stairs or in the yard or in the kitchen. We can chalk this up to forgetful workmen, noisy pipes and homeowners who are stressed to the max while pouring their life savings into this money pit. It can be "all of the above" or "none of the above".

Haunted places come in all shapes and sizes. Historical sites are big on the list. Lots of action, tragedy and emotion will congregate there that could provide a source of energy of a disembodied spirit to thrive on for a time. The shear intensity of the event that took place at the site may harbor residual energy. It does not matter to us that it is either one – we take what we can get, and we love it!

Personally, I have a map that I have created with a driving route sketched out calling it the Haunted Tour. Not that the Mister (my husband), is wild about this idea. I have already dragged him to quite a few actively paranormal places that prompted him to ask, "…why do we always end up vacationing where a bunch of people have died a horrible, violent death?" I think he is catching on. Anyway, I started a list of these places in order to sort out a couple notable ones for discussion. Once you start jotting them down, more just keep coming. There are a few that stand out from the rest; Eastern State Penitentiary, Alcatraz, Villasca

Axe Murder House – just to name a few. Internationally, there are other places such as Proveglia Island off the coast of Venice, Leap Castle in Ireland, Corvin Castle in Romania and anything/anywhere in England. Listing all the places we know to be active would produce an immense document. I have picked one that I find intriguing. Strangely enough, a significant amount of paranormal activity is and has been reported in, of all places, the White House.

It is not strange that the most frequently reported ghost in the White House would be Abraham Lincoln. He has been reported to be seen and felt by a variety of visitors, guests and residents. After the loss of her young son Willie to typhoid fever and previously another son Eddie, from tuberculosis, Mary Todd Lincoln regularly held seances in the White House. She consulted a series a mediums such as Nettie Coburn Maynard and William Shockle as well as others, dragging poor Abe with her. Abraham Lincoln is a large and prominent figure in the Spiritualist community. Was he a believer? Is it more than possible that Abraham Lincoln did not just believe in the supernatural, but that he participated in it? In my opinion, he took the process for face value. Yes, he did attend seances that were held in the White House, but Mary Todd was a force to be reckoned. Her sons were dead. If there was a chance, she could speak with them again and Abe needed to be there, then by gum, Abe was going to be there, whether he wanted to be or not. Whether he accepted the movement or not, is a fact that cannot be determined. There is a story about one particular session that Lincoln was in attendance where the medium brought through an entity that identified himself as Dr. Bamford. He advised Lincoln that the conditions and morale at the front lines were very bad and at a critical level during the Civil War. Lincoln asked what he could do to help the situation. The spirit called Bamford recommended he and Mrs. Lincoln visit the front lines and mingle with the troops to hear their stories and grievances. They both did so, and by July of that year, the Union Army were dominating both the eastern and western fronts.

There were other documented phenomena that happened to Abe. More than once he experienced prophetic dreams and visions that foretold his death. Many Spiritualists who were often guests in the White House had given him warnings about the dark shadows that hung over him. He is often referred to as being melancholy and suffered from depression. No kidding. If you were trying to drag your country through a brutal civil war, lost two children and were getting dreams and visions about your death, I'm thinking you will be feeling a bit blue.

Lincoln seemed to be most active during the Roosevelt administration. This is attributed to the turmoil of the war and the economic instability of the nation during that time. Eleanor Roosevelt, while never stating she actually saw Lincoln's ghost, stated she felt a distinct presence in various places in the White House. Winston Churchill had many stays at the residence in the 1940's. On one of these visits, he was just finishing his bath and was walking into the main bedroom, dressed only in a cigar, (which summons up some interesting images) when he saw Lincoln standing by the fireplace. "Good evening, Mr. President," Churchill reportedly said. "You seem to have me at a disadvantage." Though he handled it well, he requested different accommodations on subsequent visits.

In the same time frame of the 1940's, Queen Wilhelmina of the Netherlands was staying at the White House during a state dinner and apparently heard a knock at her bedroom door. When she opened the door, the 16th president was standing there. She promptly fainted. The Queen surprised the current President and a number of cocktail party guests the next evening when she recalled the encounter. She told them after she saw the apparition, she later woke up on the floor. By that time, the ghost had vanished.

Gerald Ford's daughter, Susan acknowledged the paranormal activity and stated she would never sleep in "that bedroom", meaning the Lincoln Bedroom. According to one account, she actually did have an encounter with Lincoln's spirit.

In 1989, Rex Scouten, the White House curator reported that Ronald Reagan commented that his dog would go into all the rooms in the White House except the Lincoln bedroom. Reagan commented he would just "stand outside that door and bark."

First Lady Grace Coolidge revealed that she once saw Lincoln standing by a window in the Lincoln Bedroom, which had previously been his office. She noted that he was gazing out the window across the Potomac to a spot that had once been the site of a Civil War battlefield.

Dwight Eisenhower told his press secretary that he was once walking down the hall when he saw a figure coming straight for him. After a moment, he realized it was Lincoln.

There are some less popular stories down through history of paranormal activity in this well- known residence. The Madisons', Dolly and James, had a tumultuous stay in the White House. The place was burned down by the British during the War of 1812. They escaped and had a short stay in the Octagon House that is also located in the Capital and has its own paranormal history. It became the Executive Mansion for a period of time while the White House was being rebuilt. It was reported that Dolly hung her wash in the East Room. She is reported to be seen walking the halls with her arms outstretched as if carrying her wash. She has also been spied in the Rose Garden, which was her creation. During Woodrow Wilson's term, there were plans to move the Rose Garden to another location. The workmen apparently reported quite a few sightings of Dolly looking none-to-pleased that her beloved roses were being disturbed. The plans were scrapped.

Annie Suratt has been heard and seen in the halls of the White House pleading for the release of her mother, Mary Surrat. Mary Surrat was convicted and hanged for her part in the conspiracy to assassinate Lincoln.

Think of the energy that has passed through the halls of this House. There is bound to be a few spirits lingering here and there. Possibly residual but possibly intelligent.

Every structure or place we visit holds an energy of its own defined by the people and events that have taken place and left their mark for future generations to perhaps learn lessons by what is left behind. For Lincoln, it may be the profound love of his country that may compel him to hang around and make an appearance during times of national turmoil.

Haunted/Cursed Items

For the most part, I have had very little exposure to this subject but feel it needs to be on the table as far as being included in types of phenomenon. Even though I am including haunted and cursed items together, they are very different in origin.

Haunted objects, by definition, are objects that are inhabited by a spirit. The spirit could be human or inhuman. It is an old concept dating back to ancient Babylon. Incantation bowls were used to capture spirits using the inscribed spell as pictured, to keep them imprisoned. The bowl was stored upside down to represent the capture. They have been used in Jewish and Christian magic practices and have been discovered by archaeologists in various places in the Middle East, so this concept is not a new one.

Pretty much anything can be a vessel for a haunted object. Previously owned objects could have a very close link to the owner and retain some of their energy. These objects could also have been used for more nefarious purposes as during performing dark ritual or conjuring and retaining that energy. Whatever your view on this subject is, remember our previous discussion about thought forms and intention.

The residual energy left by this type of use can be bothersome at the very least. It may have built up after repeated use of ritual items such as a mask, knife or other objects. It can also be linked to an entity who had a great attachment to the item and does not want to sever their connection. The entity or energy itself is not deliberately targeting a person. The unfortunate person just happen to be the one that picked it up and took it home.

Entities who attach to an item may also be gravitating to something that is familiar to them like the new owner's interests and habits. Some items that have been associated with tragedy can hang on to energy that can be distressing. It is hard sometimes to resist taking a souvenir when visiting places that have experienced overwhelming death, destruction and other catastrophic events. It's hard to tell what is coming home with you.

Early in my ghost hunting experience, the team was investigating a private residence. In addition to my contribution to the investigation, I would email my friend and colleague Anita for her input from a mediumship standpoint to compare with my own using traveling clairvoyance. Anita's information comes short, sweet and to the point. She stated she was visualizing an arm with the hand severed off of it. Well, that's pleasant. I had no input like this coming to me. Somewhere during the course of the investigation, we received an EVP that stated "...go back to the basement". So Jerry, one of the lead investigators, went back to the basement, only to find a very large menacing-looking machete that was secreted under the basement stairs!

The owner of the home claimed she had no idea it was there and could not imagine how it got there. Was this the source of her paranormal issues? Was there some connection to Anita's vision of a severed hand? There were other factors with this case so it was hard to determine, but was intriguing none the less.

Cursed objects on the other hand are created with malicious intent and designed to do harm. I once heard someone say "Curses only have power if you believe in them". I will lean to that wisdom, but only so far. Most cultures have some sort of consequence built into their belief system for handing down harm to another, but unfortunately that does not seem to deter people from crossing that line. I will bet that most families have whispers of relatives who had a connection to some sort of ethnic supernatural tradition, mine included. I have a rich Italian background. I am sure I have more that one Strega Nona in my lineage. I am hoping to be referred to one myself in my dotage.

The thing is with these traditions, there is a light side and a dark side. Curses, for the most part seem to be connected to negative emotions, such as lust, fear, envy, jealousy and the like. The perpetrator designs some item to be perhaps a gift or something mundane, leaving it inconspicuously in a person's personal space. They then stand back and watch the antics. These items can be a variety of things. Dolls are more common with the West African traditions of Hoodoo and Voodoo, as they do resemble mini people.

There are a number of famous cursed items that defy logic with the history of tragedy that is attached to them. Robert the Doll was supposedly cursed by the owner's nanny after having a falling out with his parents. Annabelle the Doll (dolls again) is the topic of the movie "The Conjuring" that was the source of a demonic haunting. The history of the Hope Diamond goes back to India where it was stolen by a priest who was put to death for his crime. There is a long line of misfortunes that are connected to it, including the death of Marie Antoinette.

James Dean's race car, "The Little Bastard" has a dark history, even after the crash that killed Dean. Parts were used in two other race cars that also met with crashes, both in the same race. Only one driver survived. The tires went to yet another car that caused injury. Apparently, the car disappeared and has not been seen since 1960.

The foremost authority on this subject has to be John Zaffis. His experience and history of dealing with haunted objects and other related phenomenon is unmatched. It makes you want to be a little more selective when visiting second hand stores and garage sales, doesn't it?

At the end of the day, what most earthbound entities all have in common is fear, anger, loneliness, confusion and/or sadness. A strong confident presence is needed to deal with them. Understanding their state of mind is essential to assisting them to their next plane of existence. We will explore that process further in subsequent chapters.

> *"The strange thing about the paranormal is that no matter how often you prove it, it will remain unproven."*
>
> *- Deepak Chopra, Indian-American Author*

Chapter 3

Mediums, Psychics & Sensitives, Oh My!

"A sensitive or medium is afforded a view of the spirit world, but only through a small hazy window. What lies beyond is often distorted and indistinct. Imagine a deaf person facing an orchestra.
They will feel the vibration of the music, discern the rhythm and pattern, but the essence of the music will always be beyond their grasp."

"Where the Dead Walk" – Paranormal Fiction
John Bowen, author

WHO WERE THOSE MEDIUMS?

On the other side of the "demilitarized zone", were the mediums who were clamoring for credibility with the scientific community. Some of them were most definitely fakes and charlatans, making it increasingly difficult for the legitimate mediums to get a foothold. Science was not making it easy.

"People do not believe they are in the company of spirits while living in this world, when in fact as far as our deepest levels are concerned, we are continually surrounded by spirits and angels."

- Emanuel Swedenborg
Scientist & Philosopher

An early pioneer was **Emmanuel Swedenborg. (1688 – 1772)**. He was an interesting figure that is credited with the grass roots beginnings of communication with the dead. He was a scientist, philosopher, mathematician, mystic and prominent Lutheran theologian who had deep faith in Christian teachings. Well known for his academic prowess in anatomy, physiology, chemistry and a variety of other topics, he began to explore a theory to find a connection between matter and spirit. From 1743-1744, he experienced vivid visions and dreams that led to a type of spiritual unfoldment. He claimed to perceive an "unseen world" while fully awake. As his abilities developed he began having precognitive experiences that were actually verified. He then devoted himself to the research and writings on this topic that planted the seed for Spiritualism. He is still revered in spiritualist circles.

A well know and colorful figure in mediumship circles would be **DD Home (1833-1886)**. Born Daniel Dunglus Home in Scotland, he was sent at a young age to live with a childless aunt and uncle. They eventually immigrate to the United States where Home came into his gift in his teen years. There were reports of rapping and tapping in the house, similar to those heard in the Fox Sisters home, and movement of items in the house. As the phenomena increased, he was put out of the house being dubbed the "Devil's Child".

Home had no problem gaining an audience. He was the rock star of his age, performing four different types of phenomena: Direct voice (ability to let spirit speak audibly), trance speaker (ability to let spirit speak through himself), clairvoyant (ability to see things out of view) and physical mediumship (moving objects, levitation, séance). He had the support of many high-profile individuals such as Sir Arthur Conan Doyle, as well as performed for the likes of Napoleon III and Queen Sophia of the Netherlands.

Subsequently, he had his share of critics, most notably the poet Robert Browning, possible due to the interesting relationship he had with Elizabeth Barrett Browning. Elizabeth was totally gob smacked with the medium, much to the dismay of Robert. It is believed that he penned the poem "Sludge the Medium" as a "tribute" to Mr. Home.

Things came to a head when Michael Faraday petitioned Home to allow him to test the medium. Allegedly, Faraday wanted Home to sign an agreement stating that he (Faraday) was not under any obligation to acknowledge any true unexplained phenomena. Home had had enough – he departed for the Continent and lived out his days in France where he succumbed to his long bout with TB in 1886.

Eileen Garrett (1893-1970) was perhaps the most respected medium of the 20th century. She was born in 1893 in Ireland; her life was filled with tragedy from the very beginning. Her parents both committed suicides shortly after her birth and was adopted by an aunt and uncle. She came into her gifts at an early

age, seeing what she termed as "surrounds", forms of light and energy around all living things (currently referred to as auras). She progressed on to seeing the dead and developed the ability to speak with them. In her early years she had no spiritual guidance and was often punished for speaking of such things. She was also plagued with ill health, struggling with TB and other respiratory illnesses.

She left Ireland for England, staying there many years, marrying often, and having four children, only one surviving. After falling ill before her third marriage, she began to investigate her role in psychic matters. During a table rapping session, she felt drowsy and "fell asleep". Upon awakening, she could see the dead relatives of the other in the room and could speak with them. After seeking guidance, she discovered her "control", Uvani, a long dead Arab soldier. Still battling ill health and a failing marriage, she became acquainted with J. Hewat MacKenzie, founder of the British College of Psychic Sciences. Eileen enjoyed a long and fruitful relationship with MacKenzie until his death in 1929.

After another bout with her health, she departed Britain for the US, seeking answers in the scientific community. In America, she subjected herself to intense testing and starting traveling the world searching for answers. She worked with many notable paranormal investigators of the time such has Harry Price, Nandor Fordor and Hans Holzer.

I like to think of her as a Renaissance woman. She was a writer, publisher, ran a hostel, opened a rest home for soldiers returning from France after WWI, founded the Parapsychology Foundation in New York City and managed to develop into one of the most accomplished trance mediums in the history of Spiritualism. What I find most intriguing about her was her no-nonsense approach to her gift, always questioning its validity. With that, she became a highly qualified researcher with respect to paranormal phenomenon. Her books chronicle investigations she participated in and assisted bringing resolution to spirits in distress.

Another well-known medium in psychical research was **Lenore Piper (1859-1950)**. She came into her gifts at an early age but did not embrace it fully until later in life. She married a Bostonian shopkeeper and settled down to living the life of a wife and mother. She was plagued with ill heath and after not finding any relief in the traditional medical community, she consulted Dr. J. R. Cocke, a

blind clairvoyant who had attracted quite a bit of attention by his unconventional medical diagnoses and cures. During that consultation, she fell into a light trance and soon after started to attend Dr. Cocke's development circle where she flourished. In her early stages, she had two "controls" or guides. One who worked with her while in trance and one through automatic writing. Once the word was out, she became in high demand in the Boston area and fell on to the radar of the Society for Psychical Research. She subjected herself to endless experiments and research and was on retainer with SPR for most of her life. She viewed her mediumship of more like a ministry than a living.

Like Garrett, she was always questioning the how and why. And, as people always do, she became victim to a misquote in the New York Herald newspaper in 1901 that casted a pall on her abilities. She was furious. She immediately issued a statement that what was printed was false. Her views became tainted like other mediums of the day who attempted to cooperate with serious research. It was always chalked up to telepathy, or ESP or anything but the possibility of actual spirit communication. She did, however, receive high praise from some of the most skeptical members of PRS like Harry Price and Nandor Fordor.

After two world wars and the Korean and Vietnam wars, a shift of consciousness was on the horizon in the 60's. The young wanted to shed the provincial attitude of the American Dream after finding it lacking. In this time, the West was looking to the East for spiritual enlightenment. It was the beginning of the New Age Movement. In the 60's, the Beatles were embracing eastern doctrine to obtain higher consciousness, dragging the rest of us with them. It led to the acceptance of many different spiritual doctrines and the development of new and edgier so-called religions that could have easily fit into the category of a cult. There was also widespread experimentation with mind altering drugs, such as LSD and psychedelics as a form of spiritual expansion.

Spiritualism was in the rear view mirror during this time, even though it was categorized as the "new non-religion" back at the turn of the century. They kept to themselves, did their thing under the radar. Enter TV...

It is hard to pin down the first medium/psychic/"whatever you want to call it" appearance on TV. There is precious little documentation on the subject that I can find, but it cannot be disputed that television has launched the career of many a modern-day medium.

The earliest TV appearance I can track down is that of Jeane Dixon (1904 – 1997). Technically, she is not a medium, but can fall under the psychic umbrella with her astrology skills. She appeared on the Tonight Show with Johnny Carson and was astrologer to two sitting presidents. She had an excellent run and had a better than fair accuracy rate.

"Death is the Graduation of the Soul."

- Sylvia Browne
Author & Psychic Medium

Another TV psychic pioneer would be **Syliva Browne (1936-2013)**. Montel Williams visited the Queen Mary with Browne on an early ghost hunt type of event. After witnessing her abilities, they formed a fast friendship, and she became a regular on his show for many years. This led to her celebrity status as a medium, author and teacher. She became a pioneer in this field and an accomplished author of many books on esoteric subjects until her passing. There seems to be a large time gap until the virtual explosion of broadcast mediumship came to pass in the last 10 years or so.

"My view of the afterlife is that it is made of different levels, depending on how spiritual a life we live."

John Edward
Clairvoyant Medium

If I had to pick one modern day medium out of the many wonderful ones who are doing the Work in present day, it would be **John Edward (1969-)**. His journey started much like my own. He was raised

Roman Catholic but stopped practicing while still maintaining his close connection with God. His mother was a rabid believer in all things psychic, and frequently had psychics come to their home to read friends and family. One of these visits resulted in Edward being read by a psychic from New Jersey that set him on the Path. He has published many books and has had his own show along with guest appearances too numerous to mention. He is know to shoot straight from the hip and becomes a bit frustrated when the sitter is not connecting with his message.

> *"People try to make it a lot bigger, weirder and spookier than it really is. I'm trying to break away from that whole weird and woo-woo aspect because I think the paranormal is more common than we realize."*
>
> *Chip Coffey*
> *Clairvoyant Medium*

Another modern-day medium I find fascinating is **Chip Coffey (1954-)**. He is a psychic medium and hails from Elmira, NY (New York is quite a hotbed of psychics and mediums). He displayed psychic ability from a young age and grew into his mediumship abilities. He is one of the few psychic mediums that work well with paranormal teams. Some of his more well-known appearances were on the TV series "Paranormal State" as well as his own show, "Psychic Kids: Children of the Paranormal" and most recently, "Kindred Spirits". He makes guests appearances on many paranormal shows and at paracons held all over the country.

> *"At death, we are aware that we are more than just our physical bodies."*
>
> *- James Van Praagh*
> *Clairvoyant Medium*

James Van Praagh (1958-) is an American clairvoyant and spiritual medium, author, producer and television personality. His career spans many years He produced an autobiographical TV miniseries in 2002 and produced the hit TV show Ghost Whisperer in 2006 that had a very good run. He has published numerous books on various psychic and mediumship subjects. He also provides instruction on several esoteric subjects through his online school. His events still draw large crowds.

There is also a good showing of the younger generation making themselves present with their mediumship gifts. Tyler Henry (1996 -) is presently the medium to the stars with his television series, "Hollywood Medium". According to Wikipedia, Henry came into his gifts around age 10. A native Californian, he graduated high school in an accelerated academic program and aspired to become a hospice nurse. After giving readings to family and friends, word quickly spread of his abilities, and he was "discovered". At 19 years old, he achieved celebrity status and was given a television show where he gives readings to different celebrities, some who he knows and others he has no idea what makes them famous. He seems to welcome the criticism that comes with the territory with no issue. When you read the lists of critics, it seems there is not a medium among them or anyone who would have a clue of how the process actually works. Some things never change.

The Ethereal Nuts & Bolts

To begin to understand how mediums can contribute to the paranormal investigative process, this area will deal with the fundamental basics of mediumship and the more esoteric side of paranormal investigation. In the beginning, I was going to focus just on mediumship in this section, but I realized that there are other types of practitioners who deal with the paranormal that do not just speak to the dead.

As I have said previously, in my early days of paranormal investigation, I went into the process with a medium's point of reference. Being trained as a medium in the traditional manner, reaching to the higher vibrations was the goal from the get-go. Imagine my surprise on my first investigation that no one was around, spectrally speaking of course. Here's the story:

On my first investigation, we were all traveling to nearby western New York to investigate a lighthouse on Lake Erie. These folks were not familiar with how mediums operated and some of the others were not too keen on the process at first. Jerry and Frank were both truck drivers by day and started a paranormal group on the off times along with their respective wives at the time.

Frank and Jerry's process at the beginning of the investigation was to do a walk-through of the site with someone who was familiar with what was taking place on a paranormal level. I had decided that I was not to be present for this part of the investigation. I did not want to contaminate my reading of the building and grounds with information that the investigators needed gathered for analysis. After sharing this with the group, they agreed, and I was banished to the outside during the walk through with an assigned guard to make sure I was not pulling any funny stuff (whatever that would have been, I could not guess). I felt a sense of real panic setting in, standing there looking out on the lake, so I told my guard, Eddie I needed to just step away and prepare myself. Talk about a mental freak out – I was very close to hyperventilation. In my head, I sent out a spiritual SOS that I was in a real fix here and whoever was out there needed to get their ass down here and help me out! This was not the traditional way I was taught to call on Spirit, but who knew that "get your ass down here" was the magical phrase for psychic assistance? It worked better than Abracadabra.

Information started flooding in at a rate that I had trouble keeping up. I strode back to the lighthouse with Eddie the guard in tow, informing the group I was ready. We had a great investigation, and I was amazed at how this process had worked for me. I felt this was going to be a work in progress, so every subsequent investigation was focused on honing the collaboration a bit more by both myself and the investigators. We developed a mutual respect for each of our contributions to the process, which I felt was the glue that held us together.

Consequently, the feeling of not sensing anyone initially was a mystery to me. After some reflection on the subject, I consulted a few medium friends and colleagues with whom I shared my views on the paranormal and came to some conclusions.

> *"The Law of Vibration states that everything in the Universe moves and vibrates everything is vibrating at one speed or another. Nothing rests. Everything you see around you is vibrating at one frequency or another, and so are you.*
> *- Unknown*

Everything operates on vibration. All things have a vibration. **The Law of Vibration** governs everything and everybody in the physical world while existing in the "unseen world". Albert Einstein figured that out with his theory of relativity in 1915, scientifically of course. The Spiritualists were ahead on that game. Awareness of this vibration could be called many things - intuition, insight, perception, clairvoyance. It is the foundation of sensing things beyond the visible world. There are different kinds of vibration that emanate from people and emotions as well as the rate of the vibration, which is a critical part of the mediumship process.

Overall, when a medium receives information from the deceased, spirits have usually made a full transition to the Afterlife. Fully transitioned folk dwell on a very high plane of existence, so you are reaching way out there and raising your vibration to make a connection when giving a reading or connecting with a departed loved one who has a message for the living. This is usually achieved by meditation, relaxation, and prayer. A daily routine of this keeps the connection fresh. You increase your rate of vibration not by speeding up your conscious mind but relaxing it. The more you are at peace within yourself spiritually and mentally, the sharper and more finely tuned you become at controlling your vibrational level and ability to tap into the spiritual world.

On the other hand, earthbound entities linger very close to the earth plane. Their level of vibration is much slower, and their energy is heavy and dense, hence when you walk into a space that is active, you feel the weight of the atmosphere kind of pressing down on you. For a medium to communicate with these entities, they need to slow down their vibration to match the slower vibration of the earthbounds. Not an easy task when you have been trained to operate at a higher level. One way it was explained to me was like becoming accustomed to using high speed internet and then suddenly having to go down to using a dial-up connection. I do not know if any of the younger crowd will understanding the dial-up reference – you can question your parents on that one.

> *"If you want to find the secrets of the Universe, think in terms of energy, frequency and vibration."*
>
> *- Nikola Tesla*
> *Inventor, engineer & futurist*

We can look at how the Afterlife is perceived by referring to the writings of Sir Arthur Conan Doyle, C.W. Leadbeater and early Spiritualist documents. The graphic below indicates there are three levels in the Afterlife that also contain sub-levels. It is believed that most people who make a routine transition usually will find themselves at the top level in the astral plane termed "Summerland". At this level, an individual is fully aware they have died and transitioned into their next plane of existence to begin their spiritual journey. The lower three levels are where earthbound spirits may reside with different levels of awareness. They may be able to still encroach upon the physical world and feel the pull of the thoughts, emotions, and physical sensations that they are not willing or able to let them go. Again, we circle back to the million and one reasons why a spirit would choose to stay behind.

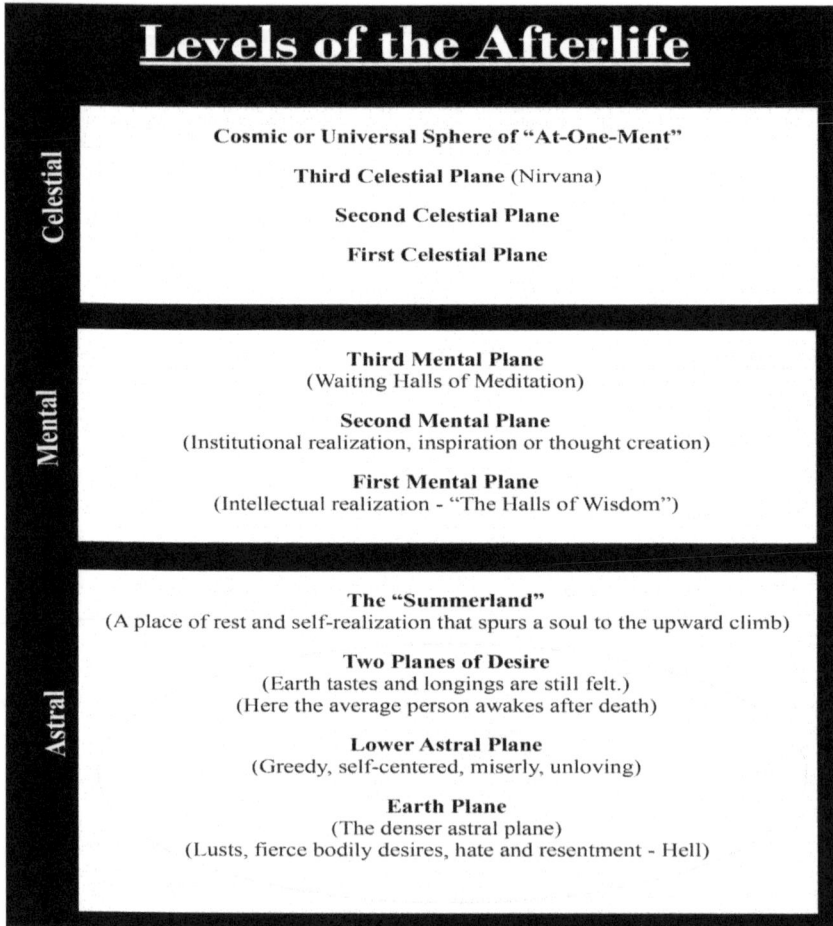

Levels of the Afterlife

Celestial	Cosmic or Universal Sphere of "At-One-Ment" Third Celestial Plane (Nirvana) Second Celestial Plane First Celestial Plane
Mental	Third Mental Plane (Waiting Halls of Meditation) Second Mental Plane (Institutional realization, inspiration or thought creation) First Mental Plane (Intellectual realization - "The Halls of Wisdom")
Astral	The "Summerland" (A place of rest and self-realization that spurs a soul to the upward climb) Two Planes of Desire (Earth tastes and longings are still felt.) (Here the average person awakes after death) Lower Astral Plane (Greedy, self-centered, miserly, unloving) Earth Plane (The denser astral plane) (Lusts, fierce bodily desires, hate and resentment - Hell)

Who Perceives What, Where and How?

There is a saying in the mediumship community that states "all psychics are not mediums, but all mediums are psychic." I find the statement a bit prepossessing, but I may be harboring some ill feelings. I had a medium once tell me that I had more tendencies towards psychic work than mediumship work. It was not meant to be constructive or complimentary. I have since deemed the comment and the medium as insignificant. It could be true – I embrace a wide variety of practices and rituals that are not totally in tune with the traditional mediumship community. However, I feel if you are not fully immersed in all aspects of your craft, your scope will be rather limited.

As I see it, there are three levels of perception in the paranormal process:

Medium
- An individual/process which contact is established between living and dead.
- Can operate on the psychic level

Psychic
- Operates on the physical or etheric plane
- Cannot translate messages from the spirit world
- May use a mantic tool, such as tarot, pendulum, dowsing rods, planchette, etc. to communicate with entities

Sensitive
- Open and/or affected by environmental changes in atmosphere (EMF, barometric pressure, geopathic stress) in any location perceiving paranormal activity.

Let us take them in turn. These will be very familiar to mediums reading this section, but they warrant review for those who are unaware or just beginning their spiritual journey. To be clear, one is not more superior to the others. All have their own contribution to the process and have their pros and cons.

"Engaging spirits is not an elitist ability or industry;
It is being active in the connection with All Things. It is innate to us all."

- S. Kelley Harrell
Author & Shaman

The medium talks to the dead. All information that is coming through them is coming from a higher plane of existence, usually from individuals who have made a full transition and have a message for the living. They receive this information by utilizing "The Clairs". The prefix "clair" is from the old French word "cler", meaning clear. These are "soul senses" that permit the medium to establish a connection with the unseen. They are briefly defined as follows:

Clairvoyance: Clear seeing

When receiving a message from Spirit, it is a visual message. This is perceived with the "Third Eye" located in the middle of the forehead. When pursuing spiritual unfoldment, part of that process is the opening of that Eye for the purpose of receiving messages. The medium may get images that are moving or still, black and white or color. Symbols may be presented as well.

Clairaudience: Clear hearing

Spirit will provide a verbal sound that is heard with an inner/soul hearing. Different sounds can be heard as well as music, speech and other identifiable noises that will help convey the message.

Clairsentience: Clear sensing

This process will deal with sensing and feeling thoughts and physical conditions. It is very similar to a gut feeling or intuition but on a more intense level. This "clair" will also assist in sensing spirits.

Claircognizant: Clear knowing

This involved the knowledge of people or events that we would not normally have that is sent from the higher planes. Information will simply pop in from out of nowhere. It could also be presented as a premonition: a forewarning of something that will happen in the future or just a bunch of information suddenly "downloading" to you.

There are a couple others that are not as common as the ones listed above, but these are the most frequently used of the bunch.

Mediums come in two varieties – mental and physical. Without dragging you too far down the proverbial rabbit hole, here are the differences:

Mental mediumship is what is commonly practiced these days. The medium is in a light trance like state and receives information with assistance from their respective spirit guides, gatekeeper or spirit team through the above mentioned "Clairs". The medium will present evidence to the sitter that confirms the identity of the spirit in question along with any messages the spirit has for them. This is called evidential mediumship. This information is viewed as subjective as it is coming through another person.

Physical mediumship is when Spirit will bypass the conscious mind and produce phenomena that can be perceived by others in a physical sense. This is viewed as objective, as it can be seen by all present. These types of phenomena were more common back at the inception of Spiritualism mostly during séance. Due to the wide -spread fraudulent practices that erupted during that time, outright physical mediumship is less common in modern times.

The flow of information between the medium and the higher planes can be a little dicey at the onset. The illustration to the left gives you an idea of how the flow can be restricted from one plane to another. As a medium continues to evolve, they can become accustom to the flow but to the beginner, it can be a bit daunting. There will be room for interpretation, which is why it is important to give as much information as possible, even it seems a bit far fetched and provided it is morally acceptable to discuss publicly (more on that later).

As a rule, mediums usually do not speak to earthbound entities. Most modern mediums do not even acknowledge them. They look upon this aspect as an old-fashioned notion that is no longer recognized by many in the Spiritualist community. As a medium myself, I cannot dismiss this concept lightly. It was something that had always intrigued me much of my life. It was also what drew me to paranormal investigation.

In my introduction I share with you my logic in seeking out an investigation team, flawed as it was. After some reflection, I began to make comparisons of processes and phenomenon between the two groups. I found some remarkable similarities:

Investigator	Medium
EVP	Direct/Indirect Voice
Orbs	Spirit Lights
Raps & Knocks	Raps & Knocks
Apparitions	Materialization
Investigations	Spirit Circle/Seance
Photos/Videos	Psychic/Spirit Photography

What is listed under the Medium column is technically classified as physical mediumship. This may be a reason that the modern mediumship community dismisses the earthbound phenomenon, but after all, the Fox Sisters had their start with raps and knocks as a method of communication.

A psychic operates more on the etheric or physical plane rather than the higher planes. They receive information based on intuition and energy coming from a space or person. That information can then be translated by the psychic into information that is relevant to that space or person. Sometimes they can perceive past, present and/or future events. They may utilize what is called a mantic tool, such as Tarot cards, crystals, dowsing rods, pendulums, etc. American mediums these days do not use these tools openly, however if you travel to the UK, mediums there are expected to know how to handle these tools as well as the mediumship end of things. I find the tools useful at times, but then, I began my spiritual journey with Tarot, so I feel a real connection with it. I do not always use them, but there are times that when I am performing a psychic card reading, Spirit will make themselves known if a message needs to be relayed.

A **sensitive** is someone who experiences acute physical, mental and or emotional responses to the energy contained in an environment or around a person. They are not able to translate the feelings into specific information, but it can be very helpful when exploring an active location. It would almost like being a human EMF meter but with more features. These folks may also have some empathic abilities which can also play havoc with their senses. They are not able to translate their feelings into actual messages but can gauge if there are changes in the environment that can be interpreted as paranormal activity. Entities can also use those feelings to impress on the sensitive different information that may be helpful to an investigation.

All three of these processes can and will be of value to an investigation. I highly recommend that if you are only practicing one of these, seek out places and people who can help you develop the ones you are not currently using. You should be constantly adding to your Spiritual Toolbox. If you are using some sort of mantic tool, I would encourage you to use them and to explore the ones that are not familiar to you. I also encourage the investigator to explore these levels of spirit communication and explore how they can contribute to your processes.

Consequently I feel that the psychic process can perceive the earthbounds best, as they potentially dwell on a level closer to the earth plane but would need to have some mediumistic abilities to translate any message or needs that the earthbound may have. Again, I stress that developing other levels of perception is crucial to the well-rounded esoteric investigator.

A Word Regarding Spirit Guides

Spirit guides and teachers are entities that inhabit the higher planes (see previous graphic Levels of the Afterlife) and have chosen to become guides and teachers to assist the living on their spiritual journey. They are crucial to your spiritual development. They may present themselves in many forms. Their appearance may be as an archetypal, symbolic representation of an entity that is meaningful and helpful to you. Some may be from past lives or may be spirit loved ones. They can be human or animal or be inhuman such as angels or nature spirits, depending on your religious bend. It can be faith based, philosophically based or anything that resonates with you. Sometimes they may have no form at all but an ethereal light, symbol or feeling of peace and love. Mostly they are individuals who have incarnated to the physical plane at least once, so they are able to understand the needs of the human condition. They will somehow resonate with you, so you are able to relate to them on a spiritual level. Traditionally, you would ask for assistance or for a guide as they will not infringe upon you without permission. The best way to access them is through dreams or the meditative state. You can have more than one guide. A **spirit band** is a group of guides that have specific roles or responsibilities that contribute to your spiritual well-being. Some key members are:

Gatekeeper/Control

This entity is kind of the person in charge. They control the comings and goings of entities and the stream of information from the spirit world. They are a crucial part of the spiritual team. If you only have one guide, this is the guy or gal you want. They can and will act as a Protector. I remember having a conversation with one of the investigators on the team and trying to explain what a gatekeeper was. I was rambling on, probably in very lofty esoteric terms, judging from Jerry's facial expressions. At the end of my tirade, he pauses for a moment and a light of understanding comes across his face and he states, "Oh, I get it – like a bouncer!". Well, yes exactly like a bouncer. For quite a while after that, when I called on my Gatekeeper, he presented himself as a big hulking guy in a sleeveless t-shirt, ripped jeans sporting a few tattoos and a dew rag.

The Gatekeeper may function as a Protector, or you may have a totally separate guide for this function. They will make sure the stream of information and energy is for your highest good and provide protection against anything coming from the Other side that is overwhelming or uncomfortable for you. If you sense emotion as I do, it can become quite difficult to divorce yourself from it in the beginning. I will still struggle with controlling emotions in some circumstances when it becomes intense. The Gatekeeper can assist in backing that emotion off that will enable to observe it without feeling it.

Teacher Guides

It is just as the title suggests – these guides are there to help you by providing guidance and information with learning situations, especially difficult ones. If you are trying to learn a new skill, you can specifically ask for a teacher guide during meditation to aid you in your endeavors. Growth and development are also within their repertoire. They should be used often. If you are wanting to learn a new skill, ask for a guide that can help you with that task.

Runner/Messenger

Again, their function is just as it sounds. Runners will bring messages and information from the realms when you are doing a reading for an individual. I have utilized them to bring in an earthbound entity's ancestors and family members to assist them in their transition to the other side.

There are many different guided meditations and classes one can utilize to find their guides. One, in particular that I found helpful was "So You Want To Become A Medium" by Rose Vanden Eynden. She will cover spirit guides and provide a nice meditation to meet your guides on a companion CD.

This chapter was to familiarize with other issues that may be pertinent during investigations that are esoteric in nature. The following chapter will deal with the nuts and bolts of the soul rescue process and the integration of mediumship in the paranormal investigation process.

"The stage is set, the curtain rises. We are ready to begin."

- Kasamari Yeswani

Chapter 4

Soul Rescue

"No one believes in magic anymore. If you hear voices in your head,
it is simply cost effective to address the imbalance with a concoction
from the drug companies. I learned that voices are not in your head if
what they say leads to a real life. If what they tell you is a true story;
if what they tell you is the ending of their true story,
if what they send you are messages that match up,
you are not mad. You are the messenger."

Helen Stavin, American Author
"The Extra-Large Medium"

Soul rescue has been in existence in Spiritualist circles since its inception back a century or so ago. Traditionally this process was performed in a seance circle where like-minded individuals reached out for earthbound or troubled spirits offering them assistance with moving to their next plane of existence. The school of thought is if these spirits are enlightened as to their true situation, they can be released from their earthly bonds to continue their spiritual journey.

The earliest rescue circles were performed in Buffalo NY around 1895-1900 by Dr. Carl Wickland who functioned as the facilitator and his wife Anna, who functioned as the medium. When forming the circle, Anna would invite the spirit into her aura and would permit the spirit to speak through her to the other members of the circle. As we discussed previously this is a good example of physical mediumship. A more modern similarity would be channeling. Both are very physically demanding on the medium, and the medium is solely in the power of their "control" or "gatekeeper". During this process, the mediums will literally "step aside" to let the entity use the medium to communicate. As physical mediumship is rarely practiced now, mental mediumship is now used to assist these souls on to their next plane of existence for the select few who still feel this is a worthwhile process. After I learned this process, it had occurred to me that this would mesh very well with paranormal investigation. Again, in the spirit of "making it up as we go along", I will share my process. This is merely a guide for anyone wanting to take up this type of work. As always, you yourself are your best guide. If it feels right, then you are on the right path.

"A lost soul often looks for another lost soul."
- Mehmet Murat ildan
Contemporary Turkish writer & novelist

How This Applies to Paranormal Investigation

To keep things in some semblance of order and documentation to be chronologically appropriate, it is important to have a process. During the pre-investigation, a more concrete method should take center stage. In teams I was associated with, one or two of the investigators would serve as screeners, setting up an appointment with the client, gathering facts and documenting the phenomena from the client's viewpoint. (See Appendix). I was never present for this part of the investigation. I wanted to ensure the information I get from a spiritual standpoint remains untainted and is not influenced by any information coming from facts gathered from the clients. I was to later find out that this method was developed by Hans Holzer decades ago. It pleases me that Hans and I are like-minded. There are a few approaches that are linked that can be used to read a location. They are as alike as they are different....

Traveling Clairvoyance/Astral Projection /Remote Viewing and More

These phenomena are all like kissing cousins. They can "stand alone", maintaining their own uniqueness but do share some similarities.

Traveling clairvoyance is the ability to view locations and events from a distance. It has been used by shamans and medicine men in early cultures. The earliest recorded case was with Apollonius of Tyana, a Greek philosopher and sage who had an episode of this while lecturing in Turkey. He suddenly stopped teaching and informed the class that the tyrant Roman Emperor Domitian had been killed in Rome, which indeed did happen. Emmanuel Swedenborg, one of the founding fathers of exploring the afterlife often experienced this phenomenon. Andrew Jackson Davis, a pioneer in the Spiritualist movement and Edgar Cayce both used traveling clairvoyance. Jackson used it to communicate with the planes in the afterlife and Cayce receiving health information on his sitting clients. With this process, information is being relayed to an individual via the seer's guides, ancestors or deceased loved ones.

Astral Travel is a process that allows a person's consciousness to leave the physical body and go to specific places, usually to spiritual realms. There are several reasons folks will engage in this process. The person is still connected to their physical body via the "silver cord" as we discussed in Chapter 2. You can read more extensively about the silver cord in the teachings of Andrew Jackson Davis and other Spiritualist publishing. This could be akin to an **out of body experience or OBE**. Out of body experience is a generic term for any situation where the spirit or soul of an individual will temporarily leave the physical body and maintain a sense of consciousness. The manner that one experiences an OBE may differ with the process that it is achieved.

Astral travel as an OBE takes place voluntarily to perhaps commune with spirit guides, self healing, to consult with the Higher Self and the like. A non-voluntary OBE would take place in a traumatic or spontaneous situation and would be classified as a **near death experience or NDE**. The sensation or experience is similar. These OBEs are finally starting to be viewed as legitimate by the medical community when coupled by a near death experience or other traumatic physical conditions that cause an altered state of consciousness such as epilepsy, migraines, cardiac arrest and the like. Astral travel/out of body experiences can take place during meditation or in a dream-like state and is viewed as more of a spiritual phenomenon or practice. Perceptions that occur are reported after the session.

Remote viewing will tout itself to be a more scientific process rather than spiritual. In 1978 the US Army established a unit code named Stargate. Its main function was to investigate the potential to use psychic phenomenon in military and domestic intelligence applications after learning that the Soviets were exploring the possibilities of clairvoyance for this use themselves. There were many sources of input down through the years such as the Stanford University Research Institute, Society for Psychical Research and the Monroe Institute. A strict set of guidelines and processes were set up for training purposes and functioned for many years within government agencies. It was later discontinued citing it failed to produce any "actionable intelligence information".

More recently many well-known people in the business/corporate sector, like George Soros, Conrad Hilton, Thomas Alva Edison and Akio Morita, the co-founder of Sony, have attributed their business success to this ability. Remote viewers will vehemently object to comparing this process with clairvoyance since while engaging in a session, the viewer remains fully conscious and can even interact while in this observational state.

Another process that has been utilized in paranormal investigation is **trance**. Basically, trance is an altered state of consciousness that allows a disincarnate energy to communicate using the medium's physical body. There are different degrees of trance. **Light trance** is a form of mental mediumship. Inspirational writing and speaking are categorized as light trance. Words and ideas are impressed on the medium by "mind-to-mind" communication. A step up from that would be overshadowing. The medium does not quite reach a trance state, but spirit energy can encroach themselves in and around the medium's aura to impress their thoughts and ideas and to communicate.

Deep trance is when the medium will "step aside" and allow a sharing of their physical body by having a spirit's energy to merge with their own for the purpose of communication. This is categorized as physical mediumship. Frequently during these sessions there may be physical changes to the medium's body such as slowing of heartbeat, altered brain patterns, and lowering of body temperature. There also may be facial changes as the connection becomes deeper. This is known as **transfiguration**. Changes in voice pattern and general manner of speech will occur and sometimes reversal of sentence structure and grammar usage. This type of trance is not widely practiced in modern times but was commonplace at the turn of the century.

Han Holzer frequently used a trance medium on his investigations and worked with world renowned psychics and mediums of their time. Eileen Garrett, who we previously mentioned worked with Holzer only once but encouraged him to pursue his work in the paranormal field. His most frequent medium of choice was Ethel Myers. Ethel would induce a trace state and channel any earthbounds or **"stay behinds"** as Holzer referred to them, to gain information regarding the haunting. Holzer would listen to the grievances or issues of the ghost and try to explain to them their current situation. When the investigation was completed and if all parties were willing, Holzer would have Myers escort the lost soul to their next plane of existence. In my opinion, this is the gold standard in merging paranormal investigation and the spiritual process for the common good of lost souls.

When doing this type of work, the type of energy and the entities who are looking for assistance will find you. Look at the circumstances surrounding your journey into the paranormal. Situations will present themselves that can lead to helping those in need both living and dead. This is pertinent to both the medium and the investigator. Those who have the need to help are drawn to the work.

I am unsure on how to describe my own process. I prefer to read a location without physically being on the premises, which is my personal choice. The experience seems to differ with each case. There will be times where the connection is deeper, and I am able to pick out minute details and sometimes interact with entities that are present. Other times not so much. Is it due to the presence of earthbound spirits or the lack of? My research is ongoing. The nearest way to describe it is a little of all the above. I do ask my guides for assistance, as always when reaching into other realms. Some mediums have a guide specifically for this type of work. I am content to use the ones that I have, but it is certainly an option to request a guide for this type of work.

Starting this process is always the same – meditation. Having a good meditation practice is essential to communicating with the Others. I feel that my meditative practices could be better. Life just seems to get in the way sometimes but sticking with it is a must for this type of work. I will not go into the nuts and bolts of meditation. If you are a practicing medium you should be familiar with the process already. If you are not I would recommend to seek out a development circle with a secondary practice of perhaps yoga, tai chi and the like to enhance your meditation skill.

Prior to the formal investigation, I am usually given an address or some general idea of where this place is. I have worked blind on a few occasions, and it worked out pretty well. I leave the logistics up to my guides. Since I am easily distracted, I try to cloister myself in an area where it is darkened, use headphones with soothing music and wrap myself in a blanket to keep from being chilled while laying still. I know it seems like a lot but at least for me, I need to provide a closed atmosphere with a minimum of distraction. After starting a meditative state, I will get to the point where I will begin to receive information perhaps randomly. Sometimes the session may be very visual. I may see a lot of detail as well as receiving "audio" information. It will feel like I am there. Other times I may just receive information in a narrative form, which is not my preference, but I am not the one "driving the bus" so to speak, so you get what you get. It is important to remember each detail as you will not know what information will prove to be relevant. I have found that small details that you have perhaps deemed to be insignificant will come out in a reveal. Investigators that do not know you or are not well acquainted with your processes will probably throw some shade on your credibility. It is understandable, so it is important to include everything, no matter how goofy.

I keep a journal of all my paranormal reads. It is helpful to look back and review your notes and recall your victories as well as identifying things to improve. A copy of this goes to the lead investigator of the group for record keeping purposes and references later during the review of evidence and for comparison with the details that were gleaned during the pre-investigation walk through.

I love the investigation. Don't get me wrong. I love using my psychic mediumship abilities, but the paranormal toys are great! Recorders, EMF detectors, Ovilus, SB7 Spirit Box – man, I love them all. My knowledge base of how these things should be utilized could use some work, but I am learning as I go. The medium needs to learn to play nice with the technology. It is your friend. Be aware that your impressions and communications to whatever is present at the investigation can easily be confirmed and correlated with the readings and evidence gathered from the technological side of the investigation. I wont' delve any deeper into the equipment side of things, mainly because I am certainly no expert, but I would encourage any medium participating in this process to become familiar with the technology and make it work in your favor.

Opening with a prayer or intention is always a good idea (see Appendix A). I mean, why not? Ask whatever Higher Power that is appropriate for guidance and to keep everyone safe (physically as well as spiritually). Ask the spirits on site, if any, to make themselves known to the group and what your intentions will be for the investigation. Some mediums ask for the ancestors of any entities to come forward to assist in communicating with anyone present. You can also request your own ancestors to ride shotgun if you wish. Personally, I have some real bad asses in my family I would not mind hanging around.

When arriving at the location, I immediately try to start some sort of conversation with whoever is there. As you continue to do this work, you kind of stick out like a sore thumb to these entities. Folks who converse with the dead give off a Light. They know you are there and why you are there. Your dialogue is paramount to their comfort level as the investigation progresses. It is also important for the medium to travel together with someone they are comfortable sharing what information they are receiving, although working with skeptics can be rather satisfying on occasion. A second witness or recorder is always a good idea.

As you progress through the investigation, it is also important to take some notes. Just as investigators will make notes about certain events during the night, so should the medium. I start off with good intentions but seem to fall short by the end of the evening. In the beginning, I was experiencing a strange feeling in my chest when I was in the presence of spirits. Initially, I initially chalked it up to a pending heart attack but after having conversations with other mediums, it seems there are a variety of symptoms everyone experiences when there is a presence.

Headache, ringing in the ears, facial and extremity movement that is not typical -each person is unique. You may also receive specific emotions spirits are trying to convey. Again, even the smallest detail is important.

Ending the Investigation

Depending on the group dynamics, a formal closing of the investigation is a good practice. If your group doesn't subscribe to this sort of thing, I would recommend doing it yourself silently. It is good to firmly state that everyone without a body needs to stay put. Your intention is the most important thing. I have included a sample in the Appendix for a reference.

Stay In Your Lane

Your asset is your attitude and the stand you take with the entities you contact as we discussed above. Negative actions, words and attitudes will fuel the situation and not in a good way. Boundaries need to be set with these entities from the beginning. Obviously, they have issues if they are still here on the earth plane. It is almost like a counseling session – you are there to find out what is keeping them tethered here and unable to move on to their next plane of existence. Some of those issues we have already covered in Chapter 2, but do not limit yourself to those topics. Each one is unique and should be treated as such. All parties should maintain a non-judgmental attitude – no screaming or shouting, no need for provocation or drama. It will not help the situation.

I remember my first private residence investigation, the preliminary interviews were complete, the investigators did their thing, I did my thing, evidence was reviewed, and the conclusion was there is was issue. Here I was at the post investigation team meeting, and everyone is looking at me like I'm the Orkin man – how are you going to get rid of this? Seriously?!

However, at the end of the day, it is the medium who is the closer here. What follows is my description of a crossing. It may not be the same for all engaging in this process, but I feel the sharing of this information is important. I call the following the Garden Variety Rescue...

How Can I Help You?

After the investigation and the evidence is reviewed, it is important to compare any information that was obtained through from the medium to any EVPs or other video, audio and personal experiences. If you can look for similarities it will assist you when you go forward with the rescue. The post team meeting is a good place to discuss what the outcome of the investigation is and if a rescue is warranted.

I prefer to do my rescue work alone. The environment is similar as when doing a remote read. It will start with a meditative process, and I will take myself to this place and open a dialogue with the entity. Below is a diagram that I have developed as a guide to the steps that I take during the rescue. As I am an old hippie, I call it the Stairway to Heaven:

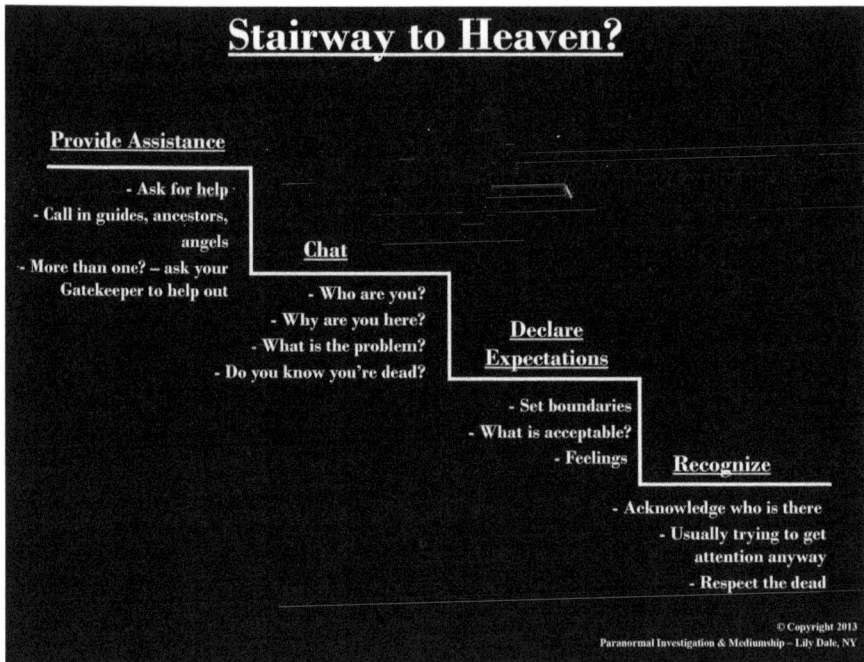

Stairway to Heaven?

__Provide Assistance__
- Ask for help
- Call in guides, ancestors, angels
- More than one? – ask your Gatekeeper to help out

__Chat__
- Who are you?
- Why are you here?
- What is the problem?
- Do you know you're dead?

__Declare Expectations__
- Set boundaries
- What is acceptable?
- Feelings

__Recognize__
- Acknowledge who is there
- Usually trying to get attention anyway
- Respect the dead

© Copyright 2013
Paranormal Investigation & Mediumship – Lily Dale, NY

Copyright Susan Stush 2014

On our first step is to recognize who is there spiritually and to start a dialogue. Be nice. They may not be so pleasant but as I said before, becoming belligerent with them will not provide a smooth process. Show some respect.

In moving to the second step, I am not suggesting being a doormat either. Firm but compassionate is what we are after. Make sure boundaries are set as to what is acceptable as far as the closeness of the connection to them and what they are impressing upon you. Your comfort level is paramount.

The third step involves getting to the root of the issue with the entity. Why are they still here? How can we/you help them? Are they willing to be escorted to their next plane of existence? There are some mediums that will try to trick the entity into "going into the Light" by telling them marginally truthful things about what they will find in the Light. I am not up with that. No one fully knows what is there in the first place. Sending them on with their issue seems unhelpful. I try to share my viewpoint of finding peace and forgiveness in the Light and let them make their own decision. I am not saying the previous process is wrong; it just does not resonate with me personally.

The fourth step is the time to call in the Light and open a portal to allow the entity to cross. If you are a practicing medium you should be familiar with this process. For me, I tap into the astral plane through my crown chakra by sending out a thread of energy and envision an opening in the darkness. As the opening grown larger, the entity's Ancestors and spirit loved ones can come forward to greet them and assist in their crossing. Spirit guides and appealing to their Higher Self is also a way to go. I achieve this by using my guides to fetch them and encourage the entity to go with them. If subsequent visits are needed, then so be it. Sometimes you do not get it all on the first try. Do not take it personal. Remember, this is not your process but theirs. If the paranormal intrusion continues, it is a good idea to make clear that infringement on the living is not acceptable.

When the transition is complete, I make it a habit to make one last shout out to any other stuck spirits who are hanging around that may wish to also move along. I was on an investigation once and noticed someone else hanging around the neighbor's property. I asked them if they also wished to also go into the Light and they agreed. It was a learning moment, so now I make it a habit to see if there is anyone else hanging about.

I close the session with a prayer (see Appendix) and close the portal.

Not an Earthbound Entity?

More often than not you will not be finding an earthbound entity. These are not common occurrences but that is not to say nothing is there. If you are a medium functioning in this manner you may be getting messages from fully transitioned spirits wishing to contact the living with a message. After all, that is your main function. Paranormal investigators who are not familiar with this process may tend to get a bit disappointed about the absence of a ghost, but I have found that a message being conveyed is just as important. There will be some sort of closure or comfort associated with this and frankly, that is the most important thing. Some investigators are up with this; others not so much.

I had this happen to me on a few occasions. The first time we were on an investigation and someone had stepped forward wanting to convey a message of thanks for being with them at their passing to someone who was present at the walk through. It turned out to be someone's ex-in-law. On that same investigation, I sensed a baby spirit hanging around. As it turned out, the owners had lost a baby a few months prior. The mom became distressed thinking her baby was a ghost, but after a heartfelt discussion, I assured her that her little one will always be close to her heart and her spirit but definitely was not a ghost.

I have found that some folks who are experiencing paranormal activity are battling some type of trauma that may be manifesting itself in a paranormal-like way. The brain and mind are pretty much a mystery to modern medicine and its capability could be endless. The modern day concept of a poltergeist is a manifestation from individuals experiencing extreme and/or repressed emotions like anger, anxiety, as well as someone who has experienced severe trauma or PTSD. In this type of situation, who know what the mind can conjure being in a highly agitated state? Frank, a friend and paranormal colleague of mine will occasionally send a case my way for evaluation on the mediumship level. There was a case where he sent me drawings of manifestations the clients were seeing in their home (it was seen by more than one person living there). As I did not sense any earthbound entities or any other presence, it occurred to me this may be a manifestation of a highly emotional state someone was in at the residence. It turned out there was.

Clearing Negative or Residual Energies

We have discussed a couple situations that may account for paranormal activity without the presence of an earthbound entity. There are times that you will encounter an area that has some "leftover" or residual energy that can contribute to the feelings of uneasiness or actual manifestations. Residual or negative energy can originate from a few different sources. Residual energy can be "leftover junk" that is somehow anchored to the area by perhaps a past traumatic event. Gettysburg and other battlefields are good examples. The energy from the events that took place may become trapped or linger. It does not interact with the living and tends to stay in one place. As there is nothing there for you to deal with you can offer a clearing if you are in a privately owned residence or space. I stress the term clearing as there is a distinct difference in clearing and smudging. Smudging is reserved for shamans and other healers of indigenous peoples all over the world.

For our purposes we will use the term clearing to avoid appropriation.

Clearings or blessings should be tailored to the situation. I will do a group participation ceremony with the family to claim the space as their own. I also use a candle that I leave with them to burn intermittently for effect. You can write your own affirmation or prayer or use one that is provided in the Appendix.

Absent healing is another process that can be used to anyone or anyplace that needs healing by sending love and acceptance. Those who do energy work such as Reiki and the like, will be familiar with this type of work. If not, it is wise to perhaps have a general knowledge of some energy healing process. Anyone can do this. Again it is all about intention. I also do a guided meditation where I bathe the area in white light and send in my "broom" to sweep out all the old stagnant energy and fill it with new and positive vibes.

Portal Hauntings/EMF/Geopathic Stress

Portals can be naturally occurring in nature. They draw and generate energy via geomagnetic energy, free flowing water /waterfalls or any number of geological phenomenon, or anything with high energy or high heat is suspect.

They can also be man made; windows, doors and mirrors can be a channel. Virtually anything can be used as a channel depending on the intention. Ouija boards, tarot cards, and things of this nature are not technically a portal. They are mantic tools that can be used to connect with spirit energy. Some feel that over time they can perhaps create a portal when used frequently enough in a common space.

If suspecting a portal, look out for odd, out of place noises, buzzing and ringing. Be alert for **apports** (appearance of an out of place item from an unknown source) in and around the area. Traditionally, apports would appear during seance but it would be possible for them to appear during a portal haunting.

If you feel you are dealing with a portal there are ways to close the portal and prevent any re-entry of entities to the location. A sample of how to accomplish this is listed in the Appendix.

EMF or electromagnetic field is the first go to for a debunk and rightly so. E-pollution in the home is an issue. Homes are being build near high tension wires and cell phone towers that generate a lot of electromagnetic energy. In addition, the amount of time we spend in front of a screen during the day is staggering, be it a cell phone, computer at work and home, television, gaming, etc. Some credit the **apparitions** and experiences in places with high EMF to this phenomenon, which very well may be true. Who is to say the EMF is not the actual culprit but is attracting the entities as an energy source? Portals or concentrations of EMF are ready made sources for energy for an earthbound. Theoretically they can be attracted to this energy source.

There are a couple of ways to deal with both of these situations.

In the matter of the high tension wires and cell phone towers, I don't believe that Verizon or AT&T will be moving them for your client. Hiring an electrician to come and evaluate wiring is also another option. Again, there is not a lot you can do to redirect running water on the property or fill in a natural gully, but you can have the client do a type of clearing that takes back their space and making it clear that their home is not a rest stop on spiritual Route 66. Planting a tree or creating a garden or nature sanctuary for wildlife is an appropriate move to honor the land. Additionally, I have found that more times than not, someone is either deliberately or unintentionally inviting things in that have no business being there. I would stress with them that this behavior needs to stop.

Geopathic stress can also be an issue. Much like the portal, it is said to come from both natural and man made sources. Some of those sources are listed above, but can also include underground pipes or sewers, any manipulation of the land (mining, quarry, tunnels and large bridges). It makes you stop and wonder how much EMF is in the air in large cities like New York and London England who have massive subway and sewer systems. These are said to cause a disruption in the magnetic field and generate those high levels of EMF that bring on the symptoms we discussed. Natural sources are things like running water, fissures in the earth from earthquake or volcanic activity, ley lines and other geological abnormalities. This phenomenon seems to be entertained more seriously in other countries, particularly in the UK. Information on this topic seems scarce as well as a solution to the situation. Some recommend Feng Shui. By moving furniture around, particularly a bed where sleeplessness is an issue, may solve some of the problem. A more esoteric solution are stones like quartz shungite and amethyst. Theoretically, they can generate negative ion that will stimulate the immune system and neutralize toxic energies into beneficial ones.

If you are dealing with a natural source perhaps a stream or running water on the property, turning it into something that will be harmonious with nature may calm the energies down a bit. A water garden or a place where birds and other wildlife can gather would be beneficial. Planting a tree or flowers that gives back to the land is always a good idea. Construct a ceremony while planting to give it as a peace offering. This has its roots with the First People here in the US and others around the world. They have been doing this for thousands of years and the fact that as a people we do not do this now may be an explanation of why our natural world is in crisis.

Elementals/Nature Spirits

I am seriously not trying to bend your mind totally out of shape but I feel the need to address some other theories that are associated with paranormal activity. Elementals or nature spirits are entities originating from the Old Religion and are a truly interesting phenomenon. In a nutshell, they are nature spirits that are said to predate mankind. They were first referred to in the written word by Paracelsus, a 16th century Swiss physician, alchemist, lay theologian and philosopher. They were also predominantly used in the 19th century Hermetic Order of Golden Dawn. The belief trickled down to Alestiar Crowley's Thelema and then to modern day Wicca. There are also commonalities in folklore and animism. Their four categories represent each element of air, water, earth and fire.

- Gnomes represent the earth's energy. They include brownies, fairies, satyrs and elves. They care for trees, flowers and other living forces that reside in the earth.
- Udines represent the water element. They include water sprites, mermaids, silkies and the like. They reside around water and sometimes may explain paranormal activity by an active water source.
- Sylphs represent air energy and are said to be beings of great beauty and have a very high vibration. It is believed they can inspire art, creativity and invention. They prefer to inhabit mountainous areas.
- Salamanders are associated with the element of fire. They have a very intense energy and fast moving. You will see this representation throughout other esoteric processes. Salamanders are prominent in most Tarot decks represened in the Wands suit. There may be flashes or streaks of light witnessed.

There are a few famous hauntings that are classified as having an elemental component. Leap Castle In Ireland is a good example. It has a long bloody history and is said to be built on a fairy mound, which is never a good idea, I guess. It was also a location where the Druids practiced their religion. There are numerous reports of apparitions of a human/animal mix inside the castle accompanied by foul odors, sightings of as well as your run of the mill apparitions of deceased ancestors and murdered family members down through the centuries.

The Bell Witch haunting is said to be an elemental haunting as well. It supposedly started with a sighting of a human/animal in Mr. Bell's cornfield. Soon after that other phenomenon began to manifest with banging, voices, music and even escalated with harming one of the Bell's children. The phenomenon was even witnessed by Andrew Jackson. After long episodes of torment to the family the activity diminished with John Bell's death but persists intermittently to this day.

Protection

I get this question a lot – do we need protection? This is one of those things I feel is a very personal decision. There are many viewpoints on this. From a modern Spiritualist perspective there is a presupposition there is nothing to be afraid of. This fear primarily stems from a cultural belief born of fear of the unknown and has not been properly represented in movies and entertainment. Also, early organized religions have twisted and contorted facts and ideas that fit their own dogma and therefore becomes controlling and fear based. Spiritualism believes all things coming from God, Spirit, The Creator or whatever you call your Higher Power, and always comes from a place of unconditional love and acceptance. However, this is where things become murky. Let me share my own feelings on the subject.

Some feel you need a positive and a negative side to things to maintain the balance. This makes sense to me and it has worked for the Buddhists and Taoist for centuries. At any rate, one should exercise caution when going into an unknown situation. Some entities are just majorly cranky and were nasty in life. They usually don't get any sweeter in death. Until they learn the lessons that life is supposed to teach them, they are not going to get any smarter or sweeter in nature. The crankiness can be misinterpreted as negative or even demonic. As for myself, I entertain all possibilities. Until you are in the investigation and can experience your feelings and impressions, it is an unknown. Below breaks down the feelings to be aware of when trying to take an initial assessment:

Discordant Energy	Harmonious Energy
• Energy drain	• Mental clarity
• Weakness	• Euphoria
• Chills	• Calmness
• Vertigo	• Happiness
• Headache	• Increased energy
• Confusion	• Feeling of peace
• Nausea	

So, if you are feeling discordant energy as described above, how do you keep this from possibly harming you or others. There is no question that caution is needed, I don't care how powerful of a medium or experienced as an investigator you are. Underestimating your target is the worst thing you can do. A firm but loving attitude is needed. Upon questioning a medium friend of mine, she likened this situation to the school playground (she is a teacher). You want to be loved and accepted by everyone and you pretty much love and accept everyone because you consider yourself a Child of Light. But looking across the playground, there they are – the bully or the mean girl. You want to extend love and acceptance, but they just are not having any of it. You need, at that time, to protect yourself and the others around you.

It is much the same with negative dis-incarnate energy. These energies or beings are lost, confused and often angry, bitter, and generally irritated. If a spirit is lost or earthbound, that attitude does not usually improve over time but will exacerbate itself. This can be interpreted many ways, sometimes that the energy or entity is evil or demonic. Frankly, if there are any women reading this who have gone through menopause, I am sure your actions and deeds were labeled as demonic at some point during that process. I know mine were. It is much the same with earthbound entities. Some may be sad; some may be angry and may lash out and cause damage due to their poor attitudes. It is everyone's job, both medium and investigator to assist these entities with their issues and move them to their next plane of existence.

In the world of the medium, calling on your Gatekeeper/Protector will assist in this process. Depending on how I feel before an investigation, I will take a few "talismans" or personal objects that make me feel safe and connected to my guides and ancestors. Like I said, this is a personal process, and you need to do what makes you comfortable. Your belief system can help you decide. It may be a crucifix or religious medal. Perhaps a quartz cluster or other stones that are said to be conducive to protection and have energetic properties you feel can assist you. It is totally up to you. Your comfort level as a medium is paramount to this type of work. It is the same for a paranormal investigator. If you are feeling out of your element or over your head, report it to the rest of the group and get the hell out of Dodge.

Many mediums practice another religion in addition to mediumship. I know plenty of mediums who are still practicing Catholics, Jews, Buddhists and Christians. I even have a friend who is a practicing Sufi. Your "protection" or level of comfort during this process can be based on whatever belief system you care to embrace. As I embrace all religions, I am comfortable asking assistance from Archangel Michael and other celestial beings that are there to help. One just needs to ask.

In conclusion, I must say I feel that this process of mediumship is a calling and something that needs to be viewed as a necessity in the paranormal investigative process. As previously stated, many mediums look at this as an old fashioned concept that is no longer embraced by the more modern Spiritualist. There are a precious few mediums you can learn this technique from these days, at least on this continent.

Chapter 5

Epilogue

Our revels now are ended. These our actors, as I foretold you,
were all spirits and are melted into air, into thin air:
- *William Shakespeare*
The Tempest, Act 4 Scene 1

As we come to the end of our exploration into the paranormal, I wanted to leave you with a discussion about the ethics of both mediumship and paranormal investigation. Even though the two processes are approaching the issue from different angles does not mean there cannot be common ethical grounds.

"My increased caution in speaking of life after death is directly linked with a
heightened appreciation of the responsibility which a sensitive,
like myself as to all those who ponder the great question of survival.
This responsibility is two-fold – it concerns those who are bereaved,
and who seek refuge or sustenance in communication with those who have died;
and those who are sincerely concerned with the significance of
mediumistic phenomena as a key to fuller understand of man's
mind and world, his philosophy, religion and science."
- *Eileen Garrett*
Medium , Author/Publisher

Mediums need to operate within the parameters that hopefully they received from their instructors and sometimes with trial and error. I know I have had my share of both, but these are learning experiences. I recently ran across an article on mediumship ethics written by Eileen Garrett in 1960. She discusses her experiences with Hewat MacKenzie and her training with him at the British College of Psychic Science. He discouraged her from the study of specific spiritual concepts as he felt there was a danger of bringing the medium's own beliefs into their readings and impressions, even unconsciously. You also will undoubtedly encounter individuals who are in a state of grieving. The pull is there to give "evidence" to comfort these individuals as they may be excessively demanding with they type of information is being communicated. This gets even more complicated if money is involved. She advises to remain detached and resist being caught up in their own grief and sentiment in order to keep your own impressions as clear and concise as possible.

This also applies to paranormal investigation. More often that not, you may not find an earthbound entity. There are other possibilities to consider, which is why the team is there in the first place. You will sometimes have an overwhelming need for acceptance that may tempt you to embellish on what is actually going on in a place you are investigating. Be upfront with everyone – if the team is worth their salt, all input will be deemed valuable. This is why mutual trust is a must.

In making a final point to mediums, personal and sensitive information may present itself during reads. Be aware that there is a time to bring up sensitive information and a time to let it pass. Just because it is given to you doesn't mean you need to give it. Or, if you are with other individuals, pull one of your teammates aside to make a note of the information for further consideration. My best rule of thumb is to ask oneself "would I want to hear this information if the positions were reversed?". Use intuition in these cases.

In the eyes of the medium, the rescue should be the end result in an investigation no matter where the entity resides. Some paranormal investigators do not think past the investigation and have trouble viewing the entities as actual people who are in need of some assistance. When investigating a private residence, there does not seem to be any issue about moving a spirit on. There is profound encroachment on the living by the dead and it is the job of the medium/paranormal investigator to settle this issue and bring the situation to a favorable conclusion.

> *"...we give out what we can as channels of Spirit. But it is up to the sitter, seeker or lost soul to receive it and take it in."*
>
> *- Judith Rochester, PhD*
> *To Touch the Soul*

In most cases there is a good outcome once the medium opens a dialogue with the spirit explaining their situation. As I stated before, tricking a spirit into crossing doesn't seem to solve much in my opinion but some mediums feel that the end justifies the means and perhaps it does. I don't share that opinion, but non the less all have their own slant. Far be it from me to judge.

From the investigator camp, I have often heard it stated by TV investigators that entities can make themselves known but there isn't anything they can do to assist them. I found this confusing. Is there really such contempt held for the mediumship process that help is denied outright? I can understand this attitude with those who fleece individuals for monetary gain, but let's not throw all of that blame at the door of the medium. There are plenty of investigative teams that are less than scrupulous in their practices. I think that ethics in general are to be looked at with a critical eye for both the medium and investigator.

I was recently re-watching some episodes of Paranormal State from back in its heyday. This particular episode was from Season 5/Episode 3. It dealt with the Old Charleston Jail in Charleston, South Carolina. Whether it was for the camera or not, Ryan Buell's concern for the spirits inhabiting the jail was virtually the only time I have seen any concern expressed for grounded spirits in any televised ghost show. The interaction with the owner of the property, the anthropologist and Buell was interesting at the very least. When questioning the owner of the property on how he felt if the lingering spirits were moved on, he casually commented that it was fine with him as he would just move on to the next haunted location.

Despite what your opinions are with the show, the topic of this episode is the crux of this book. What are our responsibilities as mediums and investigators to these lost souls? Are they to be treated as lab rats to be studied, recorded and poked at without any regard to their situation? I have discussed this with my medium friend Robin, and she likened an investigation to a visit to a paranormal zoo. Yelling at entities, recording, analyzing, throwing peanuts at them...it is like a zoo. Even so far as charging admission. Frankly I was guilty of that attitude early on. It was not until my scope of understanding was broadened that I was to consider what the ramifications of leaving these souls without some sort of assistance. Sometimes all that is needed is an offer of help. If it is accepted, fine. If not, well you can only do what you are able to do.

I understand the investigator's attitude in the matter. If they are moved on, what will be left to investigate? Unfortunately, there are more than enough lost souls out there to satisfy unending investigations. Frankly, if the soul rescue process is utilized and a subsequent investigation is conducted, it can verify the spirits have moved on, thus providing more weight to proving life after death, which at the end of the day is the point.

I feel that developing ethics within a group is the responsibility of its members as well as carving out a purpose and how the team will go about achieving that purpose. This is why I feel it is important to align with other like-minded individuals. Not to say everyone needs to have the same opinions, but just the ability to be reasonable and listen to all angles. A bit of research on ethics will go a long way. It is a given that these ethics may come into question when stumbling upon a situation that may cause a review the belief system the team is currently operating under. This is a good thing. It signifies growth and a widening of understanding. As humans, we instinctively know in our hearts and minds what is right and what is wrong. It is the choices we end up following that puts us on the scale of good and not so good.

Each of us on both sides holds crucial skills that will contribute greatly to a positive outcome. At the very least, it may present questions that were never asked before that can provide another perspective. That is true research.

It is my wish moving forward, that this book may be used as a springboard to opening a meaningful dialogue between mediums and investigators.

Good Hunting.

Glossary

Absent Healing
The process of sending energy to an individual or place, usually performed in a meditative state, for the purpose of assisting the healing process be it physical, mental, emotional or spiritual. (also known as distant healing, energy healing, chakra healing, Reiki)

Apparition
A supernatural visual appearance of a person or thing, specifically a ghost.

Apport
Objects that may materialize without physical means, traditionally appearing during a séance but may also appear at perceived haunted locations.

Astral Plane
Term coined by Bessat and Leadbeater identifying the first full level of the afterlife.

Astral Projection
An intentional out of body experience for the purpose of visiting other planes of existence

Clairaudience
"clear hearing" - ability to listen to an independent internal voice from the spirit world when transmitting a message.

Claircognizance
"clear knowing" - having knowledge of people, places and sometimes events not fully known from a spiritual source.

Clairsentience
"clear feeling" - ability to translate feelings and impressions from a source outside the normal range of perception.

Clairvoyance
"clear seeing" - ability to view information by utilizing the Third Eye/Mind's Eye

for spirit communication.

Clearing

Generic term for a ceremony that serves to remove negative energy and/or renew the spiritual atmosphere in an area.

Demonologist

An individual who deals with the study and issues related to demons and other dark energies.

Discarnate Energy

Alternate term for a spirit or ghost

Electromagnetic Field/ EMF

A field of energy which possesses magnetic and electric properties and surrounds objects with an electrical charge. A theory of unexplained EMF could be an indicator of paranormal activity.

Elementals

Nature spirits that personify the four elements of air, fire, earth and water.

Ethereal Double

An energy body of lighter less dense material that is connected to the physical body sometimes referred to as an aura.

Ethereal Plane

Level of the afterlife that represents the subtle part of the lower plane of existence and is coexistent with the physical plane.

Extrasensory Perception (ESP)

Perception of information not gained through recognized physical senses.

Fox Sisters

Sisters who lived in the burned out district of update New York at the turn of the century that heard knocks and raps in their small cottage that later gave birth to the science and philosophy of Spiritualism.

Gatekeeper

Main spirit guide that controls and monitors the coming and going of spirits, entities and other spirit guides during healing, meditation and other spiritual processes.

Geopathic Stress
Distorted or disrupted electromagnetic of the Earth that can be man made or occur in Nature.

Ghost
An apparition of a dead person which appears or becomes manifest to the living and has not made a full transition in death.

Ghost Club
Purportedly the oldest organization in the world associated with the paranormal.

Haunting
Visitation or in-habitation by a ghost.

Law of Attraction
The belief that the universe creates and provides for you that which your thoughts are focused on - "Like Attracts Like."

Law of Vibration
One of the Universal Laws that states that all things in the universe have their own level of vibration. These vibrations set up a resonance and seeks to partner with other matching vibrations. It is the basis for the Law of Attraction.

Manifestation (Materialization)
May include an element of an apparition, but could become a mixture of tangible signs of a haunting, including: tactile (a sense of touch or scratches); auditory (noises – subtle or loud); olfactory (odors and smells); or shadow figures.

Medium
An individual who is able to communicate with the souls of those who have departed the physical world.

Mental Mediumship
The practice of spirit communication by receiving information from spirits who have passed on to be communicated to an individual for validation of life after death.

Near Death Experience/ NDE
An unusual experience taking place on the brink of death and recounted by a

person after recovery.

Orbs
Balls of energy or light that are thought to represent the energy field of a spiritual being.

Out of Body Experience (OBE)
Generic term for a temporary separation of the physical body and the soul usually having a sensation of floating and able to observe people and events.

Paranormal
General term that designates experiences that lie outside the range of normal experiences or scientific explanation.

Physical Mediumship
Form of mediumship where the medium is able to produce physical phenomena (i.e. materialization, sounds, voices, trance, channeling)

Poltergeist
From the German word meaning "noisy ghost", it is theorized that the phenomenon is due to uncontrolled psychokinesis called RSPK (recurrent spontaneous psychokinesis) and is centered around an individual called an agent. It can be attributed to this agent being in a highly emotional state that may cause the phenomenon.

Portal A perceived opening or gateway to another plane of existence.

Possession
An unusual or altered state of consciousness and associated behaviors purportedly caused by the control of a human body by spirits, ghosts, demons or gods.

Psychic
A person who perceives information from a person's energy or aura.

Psychokinetic Energy (PK Energy)
Activity dealing with conscious mental energy directly affecting physical objects.

Psychometry
Process in which a sensitive individual can sense a presence or energy in a material object by handling it.

Reincarnation
Rebirth of a soul into a new body

Remote Viewing
The practice of seeking impressions about a distant or unseen target using extrasensory perception (ESP) or sensing with the mind by following a strict CIA protocol

Residual Energy
Strong emotional energy that has been imprinted from a person that is living or dead on to objects and places.

Seance
A meeting of individuals who attempt to contact the dead, usually with the aid of a medium.

Sensitive
An individual who can sense changes in the atmosphere that may be the result of paranormal activity.

Silver Cord
An energetic tether that connects the etheric and physical bodies during a person's incarnation on the physical plane and will sever at the time of death.

Society for Psychical Research
The oldest psychical research organization dedicated to the study of parapsychology.

Soul Fragmentation
A small part of the essence or soul that splits away from a person in order to assist them in coping with a traumatic experience.

Spirit
Essence or soul of a person who has departed the physical plane.

Spirit Attachment
A full or partial takeover of a living person, animal, land or object by a discarnate being.

Spirit Control   See Gatekeeper

Spirit Guide
Beings of Light that assist the living on their life path.

Spiritualism
Religious movement based on the belief of the continuity of life after death and the deceased ability to communicate with the living.

Stay Behinds
Term coined by Hans Holzer for a ghost

Stone Tape Theory
Theory that ghosts/hauntings are similar to a tape recording created by emotional and traumatic events and are sometimes "stored" in the environment. They will replay when certain conditions are present. (see also residual energy)

Summerland
Name given to the level of the afterlife that a soul usually arrives at after death.

Table Tipping
A form of psychic phenomena in which a table rotates, tilts, or rises completely off the ground by the mere contact of the fingertips of an individual or group of individuals. In exceptional cases tables have been known to move or even levitate without direct contact.

Thought Forms
An entity made of positive or negative energy and contains emotional and mental matter that can affect an individual or group of individuals

Trance
A half conscious state characterized by an absence of response to external stimuli, typically induced by hypnosis or entered by a medium.

Transfiguration
Process in which while the medium is channeling their facial features and mannerisms will be altered to align with the spirit being channeled.

Traveling Clairvoyance

The ability to perceive people, places and things without being physically on the premises.

Universal Laws

Also referred to as Spiritual or Natural Laws, are the unwavering and unchanging principles that govern the Universe.

Vortex

Swirling centers of energy in certain places that are said to generate both positive and negative energy that can affect a person's physical and emotional health. It is also theorized that it may serve as an energy source for spirit beings.

Walk-in

A person whose original soul departs the body and is replace by a departed soul.

Appendix

Sample Investigation Screening Form

Interview with:

Number of people in residence and their respective ages:

Shadows/mists/dark spots seen? Frequency? Specific time of day/night?

Distinct sounds/voices/footsteps?

Age of house and history:

Creek or water nearby?

Wiring and Plumbing– old or updated?

Who witnesses the most activity? Witnessed by anyone not in residence?

Any feeling of being watched, nausea, skin rashes, tiredness or dizziness?

Missing items that will turn up later?

Appearance of items that are not familiar

Cold spots in house?

Pets acting strangely?

Any unusual smells (i.e. foul, Sulphur-like, perfume, etc.)?

Anyone in the house engaged in ritual type activity?

Anyone in the house currently taking prescription drugs?

Recent passing of family/close friends?

House size/description:

Soul Rescue

Before Starting:
- Ground yourself
- Perform a protection ceremony
- Do whatever makes you comfortable
- Call in your guides for assistance

During the Rescue:
- Introduce yourself and anyone who is with you. You may want to record the session.
- Show some respect – these were people at one time.
- Your Higher Self may ask permission to work with the entity's Higher Self.
- Lay your ground rules – be firm but compassionate.

Good questions to ask during the session:
- "Is there anyone here with me/us? Please make yourself known".
- "Do you know that you are dead?"
- "What is your name?"
- "Are you stuck here?"
- "Do you have a message for someone we can deliver?"
- "Can you see us?"
- "Would you like to move away from this plane of existence?"

Ask your guides to bring forward the entity's ancestors and guides.
If spirit is willing, move them through the portal

Closing the Rescue:
- It is imperative to close the temporary portal.
- Thank your guides, angels, ancestors for their assistance.
- "Chillax" a bit and bring yourself back slowly.
- Document your experience in a journal in order to reflect back on your performance.
- Depending on what you are sharing with home owners, advise them not to speak of the spirit for a few days.
- You may want to sage the area to break up some of the stagnant energy that may linger.

Medium

Before Starting:
- Tie back long hair
- Wear soft soled shoes
- No perfume or strong smelling soap, body wash, aftershave, etc.
- Be sure to clear the use of a medium with owners if working in a private residence.
- Be respectful to other people's belief systems.
- May be better not to have owner present during the walk through. If you wish to share something with them, use own judgment.

Beginning the Investigation:
- Pair off - no one should investigate alone for safety reasons as well as validation of any phenomenon, should it occur.
- Take another team member to record impressions and ask pertinent questions for clarification.
- Move through location room by room.
- What is being presented to you and how?
- Use the "Clairs" – sensing, hearing, feeling, even smells and tasting.
- For those who use guides, ask them to assist in communicating.
- Be aware of signs and symbols that are presented to you.
- Take some extra batteries with you in case of drain – another possible sign of spirit presence.

During the Investigation:
- Go room by room, staying an agreed upon time
- Be mindful of spikes in EMF (electromagnetic field) and on the K2 meter, noting if they coincide with what you are sensing.
- Use judgment during the investigation whether to continue to provide input from your viewpoint. A constant feedback of what Spirit is presenting to you may become a distraction to the rest of the team.
- Discuss with team members when this can/should be shared.
- It may be helpful to revisit an area of the investigation by yourself and record what your feelings are. This can be reviewed with the group during evidence review to see if there is any correlation with other evidence collected. Always tell someone where you are going Take a walkie with you in the event of an emergency.

Prayers For Clearings & Blessings

Opening an Investigation
#1
We are gathered here to commune with those who are no longer with us here in the physical world. We come with intentions of Light and Love. We will offer help and assistance to those who are in need of it and declare our intentions are for the Highest Good.

As we prepare ourselves for this endeavor and open to this communication, we ask the God of our own understanding reside in our hearts and minds. Envelope us with the protection of the Light of Unconditional Love. We ask for guidance, composure and the ability to assist any spiritual being who is in need.

We are now grounded and open to a higher understanding and a higher purpose.

#2
To the spirits who inhabit this space which we may connect with tonight, we welcome you to guide us, teach us, interact with us. Help us connect more deeply to your world, Please allow the invisible to become visible in any way and by any means.

We are grateful and honored to be here. This investigation is opened.

Closing an Investigation
Our endeavors here at this place are at an end. We thank and honor any and all spirits who have chosen to interact with us. We wish you only peace and tranquility.

Our worlds are far apart. Please respect our space by remaining here. If help is requested from you, we will return to assist you to your next place of existence. We will not forget you.

This investigation is closed.

Prayer For Transition

We gather here together in this troubled space to offer assistance to any and all entities who reside here after their transition from the physical realm. Love is the Universal language that transcends all worry, all hurt, all hate and all darkness. Feel the Love that radiates for you in this circle. It is all for you. Embrace this Light and find forgiveness, find acceptance, find restitution, find peace.

We ask for the ancestors and guides of these souls to intercede and also provide healing and love. Envelope them I the Light and escort then to their next plane of existence.

We ask all of this with a sincere and full heart. May the Divine Presence fill this space with love and peace for all who reside here forever and ever.

Prayer For A Clearing

Into this smoke I release all energies that no longer serve the Highest and Best good. We release all negativity that invades this space and all fears and anxiety limiting peace and harmony. You have no power here. Today we fill this space with love and joy. Peace to all that reside here.

Closing a Portal

Before staring this ritual, you will need to determine where the perceived portal is located. You can use a pendulum or dowsing rod for assistance. Set up a sacred space with whatever will make you feel comfortable (ie, candle, stones, incense or burning herbs, etc). If you are doing this remotely, you will want pretty much the same type of environment. Your goal is to raise your vibrational energy.

When you are ready:

1) Set your intention for the ritual. Healing energy is needed for this work so make sure you are clear on what you are doing. You will need to remain non-judgmental towards any and all entities you may encounter and present a calm demeanor.

2) Start your meditation and ground yourself. In other words, go to your "happy place" and if needed, ask for assistance from your guides, ancestors, etc. In your mind's eye, visualize the portal as a hole or opening. Start to reduce the image a little at a time until it is completely closed. You can even visualize sewing it shut. If you are familiar with Reiki symbols, you can utilize them to heal the opening or seal it shut with some other appropriate healing symbol.

3) Give thanks to whatever guides, angels and the like that have assisted you. Reinforce that the portal must stay closed and that no entities can enter or travel from this space again. If this is a home, reiterate to the owners that no one in the house should be inviting spirits back in. There are times that owners say they are not engaging in this practice, but it can end up that someone in the home is doing just that.

Unfortunately, if the disturbance or portal is caused by a natural occurring phenomenon such as running water, geopathic stress and the like, it is possible for the portal to open again. A repeat closing may need to be done on a periodic basis.

Bibliography

Blum, Debra, "Ghost Hunters: William James and the Hunt for Scientific Proof of Life After Death"; New York, NY; The Penguin Group; 2006

Weisenberg, Barbara; "Talking to the Dead: Kate and Maggie Fox and the Rise of Spiritualism"; New York, NY; Harper Collins Publishers; 2005

Buckland, Raymond; "Buckland's Book of Spirit Communication"; Woodbury, MN; Llewellyn Publications; 2011

Clarke, Roger; The Natural History of Ghosts: 500 Years of Hunting for Proof"; London UK; Penguin Books Ltd.; 2012

Guiley, Rosemary Ellen; "The Encyclopedia of Ghosts & Spirits"; Facts on File; 2007

Fiore, Edith; "The Unquiet Dead'" Ballentine Books, 1995

Wickland, Carl; "Thirty Years Among the Dead"; London, England; The Spiritualist Press; 1978

Baldwin, William; "Spirit Releasement Therapy - Healing Lost Souls"; Headline Books; June 1995

Ingerman, Sandra; "Soul Retrieval: Mending the Fragmented Self"; HarperOne; Unknown binding; 1749

Rochester, Judith; "To Touch the Soul; How to Become a Medium"; Birmingham, AL; WaterMark, Inc.; 2016

Zaffis, John, Guiley, Rosemary Ellen; "Haunted by the Things You Love"; New Milford, CT; Visionary Living, Inc.; 2014

Conan Doyle, Arthur; "Book of the Beyond - A New Edition of Ivan Cooke's 'The Return of Arthur Conan Doyle' With Two White Eagle Teachings"; White Eagle Publishing Trust; Revised edition; 2003

Davison, Wilma; Spirit Rescue: a Simple Guide to Talking with Ghosts and Freeing Earthbound Spirits; Woodbury, MN; Llewellyn Publications, 2006

Websites

Trance Mediumship and Channeling | First Spiritual Temple (fst.org)

www.spiritrelease.org

https://www.spiritualpathspiritualistchurch.org/traveling-clairvoyance/

What Is the Etheric Body? Find Out | Imagine Spirit

https://www.healthline.com/health/out-of-body-experience#causes

https://trancemedium.co.uk/

www.ghosts101.com

Types of Ghosts - The Ultimate Guide - Paranormal School

www.wellwholeempowered.com/blog/2020/2/walk-ins-why-some-souls-choose-to-hand-over-the-wheel

www.supernaturalmagazine.com/spirit-portals-and-energy-vortexes

https://paranormalschool.com/elemental-spirits-complete-guide/

https://fst.org/spiritual-teachings/the-ethics-of-mediumship/

https://theghostinmymachine.com/2020/03/09/how-does-it-work-the-stone-tape-theory-residual-hauntings-and-the-deep-influence-of-memory-and-emotion/
https://ss-times.com/what-is-the-difference-between-an-apparition-and-a-manifestation/

Workshops

Stush, S. "Mediumship & Paranormal Investigation: A Spiritual Collaboration:, August 2014, Lilydale NY, PPT Presentation

Stush, S. "Diversity in the Afterlife", October 2017, Edinboro University of Pennsylvania, Edinboro PA, PPT Presentation

Acknowledgements

Please know this book is not the "be-all-end-all" guide to mediumship in paranormal investigation. Its purpose is to share information with developing mediums who wish to pursue soul rescue and for paranormal investigators to more fully understand how a medium can contribute to an investigative process and provide an overview of what they do. There are a lot of question marks throughout, as in my opinion, this whole process is one giant question mark. If you are not asking questions and considering the whole enchilada, your research will be flawed, hence the question marks.

I hardly know where to begin because so many people contributed to this process. First and foremost, my Spirit family was established so long ago in Lily Dale; the "Gang of New York", Anita, Robin, Cindy, Cecelia, Brenda, Jill, Barbara Ann, Dorothea, Pamela, Linda, and scores of others down through the years. Foremost, my mentor and teacher, Dr. Judith Rochester, guided us down the path of Spirit, sometimes kicking and screaming. Her support and acceptance can never be measured. She is truly the Medium's Medium.

On the other side of things is my "Ghost Family" – there have been a couple. Billy, Katie, Jerry, Frank, Eric, Lindsey, and others. You know they are family when your reading on a place that is so far off base. It may as well be on Mars, but they kindly look the other way and twist it so it doesn't look so bad. It was such a fun ride and at times, goofy to the nth degree. It was, surely, some of the best of times on this plane of my existence.

I would also like to include Dr. Salene Cowher who held my feet to the fire and offered both technical and emotional support during the times I felt this would never come to pass.

Finally, to all those mediums who gave me readings over the years and kept telling me I was going to write a book. This is paying it forward, to boost your accuracy level (joke).

About The Author

Susan Stush is a medium, tarot card reader, non-denominational ordained minister, and paranormal investigator. Her journey into the paranormal has produced a growing fascination and commitment to both the paranormal and Spiritualist experiences. She has enjoyed "the hunt" with different area paranormal groups while learning the fine nuances of mediumship at the knee of mediums trained in the traditional fashion. In her professional experience, she functioned as an administrative assistant in the healthcare and cancer treatment arenas as well as in higher education. She was exposed to a diverse population that aided in the development of her mediumship and investigative abilities, often finding folks at her office door with their paranormal issues. She has earned a dubious reputation as having a "Queen of the Undead" thing going on.

She strives to bridge the gap between the living and the dead, assisting with both their needs and where they need to be. Susan has lectured on various paranormal topics in the Pennsylvania and Western New York areas, as well as Toronto, Canada. She has also appeared on podcasts, A1R radio, and YouTube, discussing the paranormal, tarot, and other esoteric subjects.

She is a lifelong resident of Erie, PA.

thextralargemedium@gmail.com

www.ingramcontent.com/pod-product-compliance
Lightning Source LLC
Chambersburg PA
CBHW050843270326
41930CB00019B/3448